Guide to SAP® In-House Cash (IHC)

Mary Loughran
Lennart B. Ullmann

Thank you for purchasing this book from Espresso Tutorials!

Like a cup of espresso coffee, Espresso Tutorials SAP books are concise and effective. We know that your time is valuable and we deliver information in a succinct and straightforward manner. It only takes our readers a short amount of time to consume SAP concepts. Our books are well recognized in the industry for leveraging tutorial-style instruction and videos to show you step by step how to successfully work with SAP.

Check out our YouTube channel to watch our videos at
https://www.youtube.com/user/EspressoTutorials.

If you are interested in SAP Finance and Controlling, join us at
http://www.fico-forum.com/forum2/
to get your SAP questions answered and contribute to discussions.

Related titles from Espresso Tutorials:

► Lennart B. Ullmann & Claus Wild: Electronic Bank Statement and Lockbox in SAP® ERP
http://5056.espresso-tutorials.com

► Ann Cacciottolli: First Steps in SAP® Financial Accounting (FI)
http://5095.espresso-tutorials.com

► Ann Cacciottolli: First Steps in SAP® FI Configuration
http://5137.espresso-tutorials.com

► Janet Salmon & Claus Wild: First Steps in SAP® S/4HANA Finance
http://5149.espresso-tutorials.com

► Reinhard Müller, Frank Rothhaas: Practical Guide to SAP® FI-RA—Revenue Accounting and Reporting
http://5174.espresso-tutorials.com

Mary Loughran, Lennart B. Ullmann
Guide to SAP® In-House Cash (IHC)

ISBN:	978-1-985362-24-6
Editor:	Karen Schoch
Cover Design:	Philip Esch
Cover Photo:	fotolia.com #89345883 © Julien Eichinger
Interior Design:	Johann-Christian Hanke

All rights reserved.

1st Edition 2018, Gleichen

© 2018 by Espresso Tutorials GmbH

URL: *www.espresso-tutorials.com*

Feedback
We greatly appreciate any kind of feedback you have concerning this book. Please mail us at *info@espresso-tutorials.com*.

Table of Contents

Preface

Although SAP's In-House Cash (IHC)[1] module has been available for many years, there is a lack of non-SAP material documenting the functionality included in the module. This tutorial is meant to give business users, SAP support and SAP consultants an introduction to the functionality included in SAP's In-House Cash module, as well as the many benefits of implementing an in-house bank. It is also meant to be an introduction to the IHC module's processes and a guide to be referenced when starting an SAP IHC implementation.

The book starts gradually, by first introducing the topic of an in-house bank and its benefits. It covers an example scenario on which the processes and configuration in this book are based. After a high-level review of the supported scenarios, it then outlines the different types of master data required. Each of the scenarios is then described in detail.

The example scenario in this book is not meant to represent a full, real-life IHC implementation, but instead shows how SAP's IHC module works, what scenarios it supports, and how it can fit into an existing SAP productive environment.

The final chapters of this book contain tips, tricks, and other useful information such as how to resolve specific errors if encountered, a definition of terms, and relevant transaction code listings.

We sincerely hope you find this book useful.

A special thank you goes to Praveen Gupta, Tim Loughran, and everyone at Espresso Tutorials who made this book possible.

---

[1] See Section 10.1.2.

We have added a few icons to highlight important information. These include:

Tips

Tips highlight information that provides more details about the subject being described and/or additional background information.

Examples

Examples help illustrate a topic better by relating it to real world scenarios.

Attention

Attention notices highlight information that you should be aware of when you go through the examples in this book on your own.

Finally, a note concerning the copyright: all screenshots printed in this book are the copyright of SAP SE. All rights are reserved by SAP SE. Copyright pertains to all SAP images in this publication. For the sake of simplicity, we do not mention this specifically underneath every screenshot.

1 In-house bank overview

In this introductory chapter, we define what is meant by an in-house bank (IHB) and the benefits of implementing one. In addition, we cover the types of organizations that would benefit most when implementing an in-house bank. This chapter is completed with a list of factors that should be considered before starting an in-house cash (IHC) implementation.

1.1 Overview of in-house banks (IHBs) / payment factories

SAP's IHC solution is a well-designed, integrated module for payment processing. Before getting into the details of SAP's IHC solution, let's briefly cover the topic of an in-house bank.

In simplest terms, an in-house bank is a way for a company to move payment-related processing – normally done at external banks – to within the company's infrastructure, and in the process, reduce external banking costs and improve controls.

An in-house bank is an organizational unit within a corporation that performs many of the financial services typically provided by an external commercial bank. Services include payment processing of both inter-company and external payments, payments on behalf of and collections on behalf of. Subsidiaries of the corporation hold accounts with the in-house bank, rather than at an external bank, giving greater visibility over account balances and greater control over processes. The in-house bank can manage inter-company loans and perform foreign exchange transactions and liquidity management processes for the subsidiaries that have accounts at the in-house bank.

Keep in mind that implementing any in-house bank requires changes in internal processes. Strong project management and SAP resources are required because of the inherent coordination required across different departments of an organization.

The terms "shared-service centers" (SSCs), "in-house banks", and "payment and collection factories" are different things but the differences between them can be unclear. In addition, people may have different ideas of what exactly they mean. All three provide lower costs, centralized processes, and reduced risks. All three involve centralizing repetitive payment processes, and all three can be implemented in SAP using SAP's IHC solution.

For many organizations, payment processing is handled within each country or region of operation, leading to costly and often duplicate efforts across the group organization. In addition, companies often have multiple banking systems, inconsistent processes, and a general lack of visibility across payment processing for the group organization. These are areas where SAP's IHC solution may be a good fit.

1.2   Benefits of using an in-house bank / payment factory

Benefits of implementing SAP's IHC solution are listed below.

Lower external bank costs:

- ▶ provide internal economies of scale leading to lower headcount, and lower IT and overhead costs.
- ▶ reduce the volume of payments made by netting payment flows across subsidiaries at the IHB.
- ▶ reduce the number of banking relationships.
- ▶ reduce external bank accounts and bank fees.
- ▶ convert cross-border payments and collections into local transactions.
- ▶ improve foreign exchange spreads from the consolidation of payments.

Better utilization of available funds:

- ▶ centralizes processes.
- ▶ streamlines payment processes.
- ▶ harmonizes payment and collection processes.

Risk mitigation from increased visibility and control:

▶ provides visibility over internal payments and control over funding arrangements leading to optimization of liquidity.

▶ reduces transaction volume across all workstreams.

▶ provides easier reporting for internal and regulatory purposes because payment information has been centralized.

▶ reduces fraud through process management, visibility, and implementation of control policies.

▶ consolidates supplier visibility enabling more efficient supply chain management.

▶ enables stronger internal controls over payment processing.

1.3 Types of organizations that could benefit from an in-house bank / payment factory

In this section, we outline the types of organizations that can benefit from an IHB or payment factory. Below are characteristics of companies that can benefit from an IHC:

▶ currently have decentralized payment processing

▶ multi-national organizations

▶ legal entities in countries that allow the in-house bank functionality (In most European countries, in-house banking is allowed. In many Latin American countries, in-house banking is restricted. Asia has key countries that have restrictions, but gradually, the restrictions are being reduced).

▶ large number of external bank accounts

▶ high number of intercompany settlement payments

▶ companies with subsidiaries that do business with the same external party across countries

1.4 Factors to consider when implementing an IHB

Before getting started on the IHC functionality within SAP, it is important to have a clear understanding of the requirements, and what is to be implemented. The below points are questions that should be considered before or at the initial stages of implementing an in-house bank. The list is not meant to be exhaustive, but instead gives a sample of key aspects of the scope of an IHC project in SAP.

▶ What are the company codes (subsidiaries) that will participate in the IHB?

▶ What are the country-specific legal and tax requirements impacting these company codes, and is the structure approved by the legal department?

▶ What are the types of payments that will be made from the IHB? (e.g. urgent cross-border and domestic payments, non-urgent payments, checks?)

▶ What bank accounts will be used by the IHB? In which currencies? In which countries will the external bank accounts be located? What is the liquidity structure or funding model to be used with the IHB?

▶ Will the bank area charge fees on transactions sent through the IHB? If so, what types of fees?

▶ What are the rules in the different countries for allowing payments/collections on behalf of?

▶ What are the tax implications of an in-house bank?

▶ Should some entities continue to make local payments or collections?

▶ Should there be a phased rollout of the payment processes supported by the in-house bank?

▶ Should only outgoing payments, only incoming payments, or both, be centralized?

▶ Where are the company's suppliers/vendors located?

▶ Where are the company's customers located?

▶ Should any of the current tasks remain with the local entities?

▶ Which payments/collections should be included?

- ▶ How many external banks should be used for the IHB's external payments?

- ▶ Where should the in-house bank be located? Should there be regional IHBs or just one global in-house bank?

- ▶ How can the existing relevant bank relationships, accounts, payments/collections, bank interfaces be leveraged when implementing SAP's IHC module?

- ▶ What is the scope of the project? (e.g. geographies and business units in scope, scope of change in processes, staff numbers/location, intercompany activity?)

- ▶ What connectivity and payment file formats will be used?

- ▶ Is the company ready to support the process changes? (e.g. changes in technology required, ability to support changes in desired timelines, conflicting projects or cultural hurdles such as local business unit autonomy?)

- ▶ What is the legal status of "on-behalf-of payments" in the relevant countries?

- ▶ What are the reporting requirements needed with the in-house bank?

2 Introduction to SAP's In-House Cash module

In this chapter, we introduce how SAP's IHC module fits into an organization that is running SAP, and introduce some of the terminology used in SAP's IHC module.

2.1 In-House Cash overview

The In-House Cash module is part of SAP's broader Treasury offering. As shown in Figure 2.1, the IHC module falls under Payment Factory in the Payments and Bank Communications portion of the Treasury Management solution map.

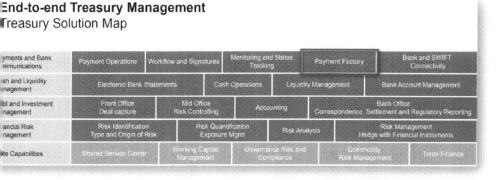

Figure 2.1: SAP Treasury solution map

SAP's IHC module supports the following processes, which are focused on in this book:

▶ centralized payments – also known as payments on behalf of (POBO)

▶ intercompany payments

▶ centralized receipts – also known as receivables on behalf of (ROBO)

▶ manual payments

▶ end-of-day processing

First, a high-level description of the functionality of these five IHC processes is given. Next, the master data related to the IHC module is outlined in detail. This is followed by Chapter 5 which details each of the five IHC processes, showing screenshots in SAP as well as additional information about these processes. Chapter 6 walks through the accounting entries for the examples described in Chapter 5. Chapter 7 outlines the SAP configuration required for the company codes where the subsidiary has an account at the in-house bank. Chapter 8 describes the key configuration for the in-house bank. The next chapter shows how to resolve typical issues encountered when testing the IHC functionality. This book finishes up with a chapter on tips and guidance when encountering errors during implementation of the IHC module, as well as a listing of the IHC transaction codes.

There is an additional process known as cash pooling, which is also supported by the IHC module, but is not covered in further detail in this book. Cash pooling involves aggregating the balances of several bank accounts at an external bank. The IHB is notified of the movement of funds when the external bank statements are processed in SAP, at which time the IHB posts the cash movements to the participants' current accounts. Cash pooling is supported by using the note to payee text in the external bank statements to determine the correct IHB current account.

2.2   In-House Cash landscape

With SAP's In-House Cash module, companies can create a virtual house bank within their organization. The organizational units involved in an IHC implementation are the subsidiaries that have at least one current account at the in-house bank, and the legal entity where the in-house bank resides. A current account is the name given to a bank account at the in-house bank. A current account and virtual account are the same thing. Throughout this book, we use the terms current account and virtual account interchangeably. Please refer to Section 10.1.2 Definition of Terms, in Chapter 10.

The in-house bank is created as a house bank in SAP, and the current (bank) accounts at the in-house bank are created as house bank accounts in the subsidiary company codes. Payments are sent between the subsidiaries and the in-house bank, and the in-house bank sends bank statements to the subsidiaries. External bank accounts are necessary and are used by the in-house bank for centralized outgoing and incoming payments.

Figure 2.2 outlines the landscape of the IHC module. As the reader of this book will see, the beauty of the IHC module is how it fits in so well with existing Accounts Receivable (AR), Accounts Payable (AP), and bank statement functionality in SAP.

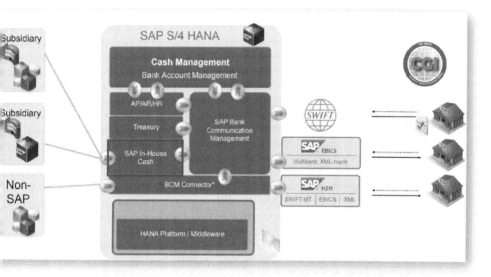

Figure 2.2: Landscape of SAP's IIHC module

One last important point to mention regarding implementing SAP's IHC module is that the module can be implemented either with the initial SAP implementation, or after a company is already live in SAP. This is because implementing an in-house bank fits into productive company codes just like adding a new house bank would. The difference is that the new house bank is an internal house bank as opposed to an external house bank.

2.3 Example scenario

In this section, we outline the example scenario on which the configuration and accounting entries in this book are based. The example scenario was selected to show the reader the basic functionality of SAP's IHC module, and is not meant to be representative of an actual SAP IHC implementation.

In the example scenario, there is one IHC center located in Belgium. The bank area is defined as "IHC" for our example. The in-house bank resides and posts to the SAP general ledger under company code 3010. Keep in mind that it is possible to configure SAP's IHC module to have multiple bank areas globally.

Table 2.1 shows our sample corporate group's subsidiaries that have current accounts at the in-house bank (bank area IHC). In our example, each subsidiary has one current account at the in-house bank, and the account is in the local currency of the subsidiary. Note that it is possible for subsidiaries to have multiple current accounts at the in-house bank.

Company code	Company code name	Ctry	Business partner	IHC current account
2100	IDES Portugal	PT	SUB_2100	SUB_2100_EUR
2300	IDES Spain	ES	SUB_2300	SUB_2300_EUR
2500	IDES Netherlands	NL	SUB_2500	SUB_2500_EUR
2900	IDES Sweden	SE	SUB_2900	SUB_2900_SEK
3000	IDES U.S.	US	SUB_3000	SUB_3000_USD

Table 2.1: IHC participating entities

The following are the AP payment methods that are defined as IHC payment methods. These payment methods need to be configured in the subsidiary company codes listed in Table 2.1.

AP IHC Payment Methods (F110):

- ▶ I – IHC Intercompany Settlement
- ▶ J – Payment via IHC (external)

The following are the more common Treasury payment methods that are used when the in-house bank makes payments. These payment methods need to be configured only in the company code to which the in-house bank is assigned, which in our case is company code 3010. (Note: the formal name for transaction code F111 is the Payment Program for Payment Requests, but we refer to the program as the Treasury payment program throughout this book.)

Treasury/IHC Payment Methods (F111):

- ▶ 1 – IHC Domestic Wire
- ▶ 2 – IHC Local Payments (ACH/SEPA/BACS)
- ▶ 3 – IHC Cross-Border Wire

Payments sent through SAP's IHC module are referred to as payment orders. Payment order transaction types are the different types of IHC payment orders used; for example, there can be internal payment orders such as IPD, which do not generate an external payment, and external payment orders where a payment is sent to an external bank by the in-house bank, such as XPD.

SAP refers to payment orders created by running the AP payment program as "payment orders generated automatically", versus payment orders that are manually entered at the in-house bank as "payment orders generated manually".

A payment order is an IHC subledger transaction that is not posted to the SAP general ledger until the end-of-day processing steps are run. The end-of-day processing steps include the activities to finalize the IHC activity for a day, such as posting the balances of the IHC current accounts to the SAP general ledger, calculating interest and other fees, as well as creating and generating daily bank statements. Any payments received by the in-house bank after end-of-day processing is run roll into the next business day.

Figure 2.3 shows the different types of payment orders used in the examples in this book. Like a G/L posting, a payment order consists of debit and credit payment items. Keep in mind that the payment order transaction types are driven by the IHC configuration.

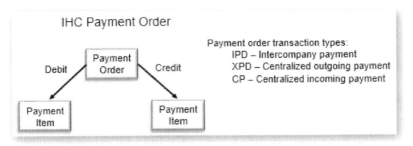

Figure 2.3: Payment order types

Table 2.2 describes the types of payment orders that are used in the examples outlined in this book. The TRANSACTION TYPE is the type of payment order. The BUSINESS TRANSACTION CODE (BTC) is the code used in the IHC bank statements for the type of payment order payment item. The usage column outlines how the payment order is used.

Transaction type	Description	BTC	Usage
IPD	I/C Monthly netting payment	020 (debit side) 051 (credit side)	Used when running the AP payment program with payment method I. Also used for manual payment orders.
XPD	Payment on behalf of	020	Used when running the AP payment program with payment method J. Also used for manual payment orders.
CP	Incoming payment on behalf of	051	Used for centralized incoming payment orders.

Table 2.2: Payment order types used for example scenario

There are three external bank accounts that the in-house bank uses for its payments. These bank accounts are used for centralized outgoing and incoming payments. They are listed in Table 2.3. Note that for each of these bank accounts, a corresponding IHC current account has been created.

The naming convention used for the house bank and account ID is the following:

House bank ID:

- ▶ The first 3 digits of the house bank indicate the external bank.
- ▶ Digits 4 and 5 of the house bank ID are the two-character country code of the bank branch where the account is located.

Account ID:

- ▶ The first 2 digits are the first two characters of the currency.
- ▶ The last three digits are the account number.

Company code	House bank	Account ID	G/L account	Currency	Account number
3010	CITGB	EU845	113400	EUR	18349845
3010	CITUS	US987	113500	USD	18349987
3010	CITGB	JP989	113600	JPY	18349989

Table 2.3: In-house bank's external bank accounts

3 Scenarios supported by SAP's IHC module

In this chapter, we describe the main scenarios supported by SAP's IHC module, from a process perspective. For each scenario, the process flow is introduced at a high-level. Chapter 5 covers the same five scenarios in detail, with SAP screenshots.

Be aware that the figures presented in this chapter may be somewhat oversimplified in that there may be some countries that, due to restrictions, cannot participate in the in-house bank; these are not displayed in the figures in this chapter.

3.1 Payments on behalf of – process flow

A very common use of an in-house bank is to make centralized outgoing payments for a corporate's subsidiaries. These payments are also referred to as payments on behalf of (POBO payments). The benefits of this scenario are that the subsidiaries do not need to hold external bank accounts, or can hold fewer external bank accounts, thus reducing bank fees for the corporate group. There are also benefits related to the centralization of external payment processing at the in-house bank.

Figure 3.1 shows what the payment structure would look like before centralizing payments with an in-house bank.

After implementing an in-house bank, payments to the same vendors across subsidiaries can be combined into one payment from the in-house bank. Because payments are being centralized, fewer external bank accounts are needed. In addition, with centralized payment processing, the number of internal payment processing staff can typically be reduced. Figure 3.2 shows a simplified example of how the payment structure for this company could change with an in-house bank.

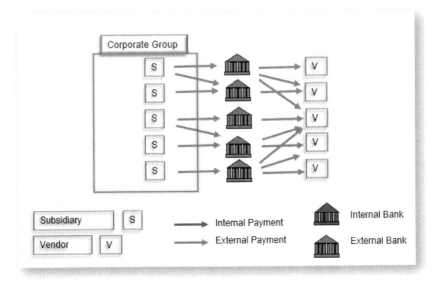

Figure 3.1: Before implementing payment on behalf of

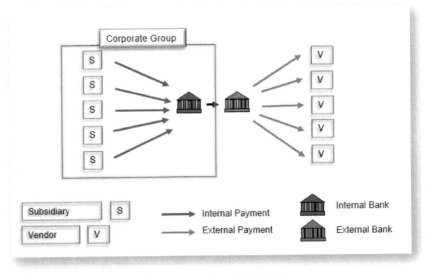

Figure 3.2: After implementing payments on behalf of

Table 3.1 describes the steps in SAP when making a centralized payment using the IHC module. In our example, subsidiary 2100 initiates a vendor payment through the in-house bank. Except for Step 10, all steps would typically be run on the same day.

Step	Description
1	The first step is for the subsidiary to enter the vendor invoice into SAP. The payment method in the invoice or in the vendor master should be an IHC-enabled payment method. In our example scenario, this is payment method J.
2	Subsidiary 2100 initiates the AP payment program (transaction code F110), which clears the AP invoice and makes a credit entry to the IHC clearing account.
3	When executing the create payment medium step in the AP payment program, a payment is sent from the subsidiary to the in-house bank. The form of the payment is an SAP IDoc (intermediate document), which is sent electronically in SAP.
4	The in-house bank receives the payment from subsidiary 2100, and creates a payment order. When the payment order is posted, the current account of subsidiary 2100 is debited and a payment request, for payment from the in-house bank to the subsidiary's external vendor, is created.
5	The Treasury payment program is run for the IHC payments. The payment request created in Step 4 is cleared.
6	When the Treasury payment program is run for the IHC payments in the step above, a payment file is generated and is sent to the bank. The payment file contains the payment to the subsidiary's vendor.
7	The external bank pays the vendor.
8	When the IHC end-of-day process is run, an internal bank statement is sent from the in-house bank to the subsidiary, and the current day's activities are posted to the SAP general ledger of the company code where the in-house bank resides. The internal bank statement holds the activity for the corresponding IHC current bank accounts for the previous day.
9	Internal bank statements are posted to the subsidiaries' SAP general ledger.
10	On the next business day, the in-house bank's external bank statement is processed in SAP under the in-house bank's company code, and it records the cleared payment sent on behalf of the in-house bank to subsidiary 2100's vendor.

Table 3.1: Process steps for IHC centralized payments

Figure 3.3 shows a diagram of the ten steps described above.

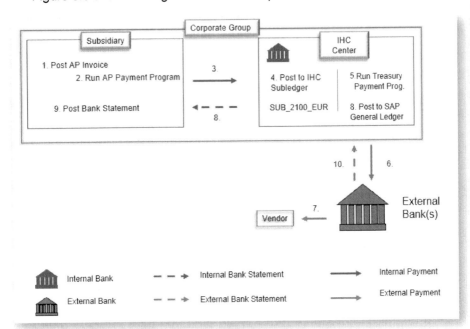

Figure 3.3: Process steps for payments on behalf of Intercompany payments process flow

3.2 Intercompany payments process flow

Another very common use of an in-house bank is to make intercompany payments.

For each combination of company codes making intercompany payments, assuming neither company code has restrictions in participating in an in-house bank, there are no external payments generated as part of the intercompany settlement process. The paying entity's in-house bank current account is debited, and the receiving entity's in-house bank current account is credited. This is referred to as a cashless payment because no external payment is generated. Making intercompany payments through an in-house bank greatly reduces the payment costs related to the intercompany settlement process because external payments are significantly reduced.

An SAP customer can go from bi-lateral netting (making intercompany payments where combinations of company codes send payments directly to the other company codes, as in Figure 3.4) to multi-lateral netting (where for each company code only one payment is made in the intercompany netting process, and that payment is either to or from the inhouse bank, as in Figure 3.5). Note: netting occurs at the in-house cash current account level as payment orders are aggregated.

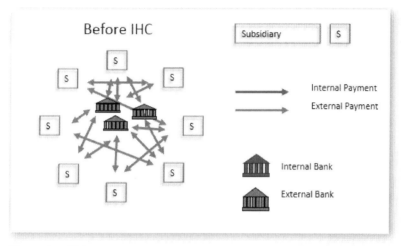

Figure 3.4: Bi-lateral netting before use of IHC module

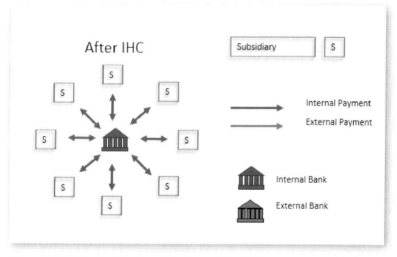

Figure 3.5: IHC subsidiaries settle through the IHB

With SAP's IHC module, companies can achieve multi-lateral netting, and most intercompany settlement payments are settled through the in-house bank. If intercompany settlements are paid by wire transfer, then using an in-house bank can provide significant savings in both time (the Treasury department's staff), and money (bank charges). A multi-lateral system is much more efficient. Below are several of the efficiencies gained when using an in-house bank for intercompany settlements:

▶ reduced volume of IC transfers (as settlement is through a current account)

▶ less time and effort to process payments

▶ reduced workload for multiple workstreams (Accounting and Cash Management) from process simplification and automation

▶ lower bank fees

The diagram in Figure 3.6 shows the process flow of intercompany payments when the IHC module is used. Note: this assumes that there are no restrictions to using an in-house bank for intercompany settlements in the countries involved.

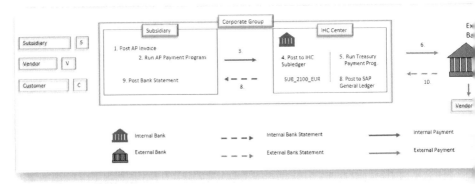

Figure 3.6: Intercompany payments process flow

Table 3.2 describes the steps in SAP when making an intercompany payment using the IHC module. In our example, subsidiary 2300 delivers services to subsidiary 2100, after which subsidiary 2100 initiates a cash-less intercompany payment to subsidiary 2300 through the in-house bank.

30

Step	Description
1	Subsidiary 2300 delivers services to subsidiary 2100. Subsidiary 2300 enters the AR invoice into SAP, and sends it to subsidiary 2100 for payment.
2	Subsidiary 2100 enters the AP invoice into SAP. Payment method I is used in the AP invoice; this payment method is used in the case of intercompany netting.
3	On the agreed netting day, subsidiary 2100 initiates an internal settlement using the AP payment program. This sends payment details to the in-house bank for processing, and at the same time the IC payable is cleared. The accounting entries made under company code 2100 when the AP payment program is run are a debit to the intercompany vendor representing subsidiary 2300 and a credit to the IHC cash clearing account.
4	When the in-house bank processes the payment from subsidiary 2100, it determines that the payment is an internal payment, and so debits the current account of subsidiary 2100 and credits the current account of subsidiary 2300 in the amount of the payment.
5	The in-house bank's end-of-day process runs, during which an internal bank statement is sent from the in-house bank to each of the subsidiaries and contains activity processed at the IHB for the day. A second action that takes place when the IHC end-of-day process is run is the posting of that day's IHC activity to the SAP general ledger of the company code where the IHB resides, which is company code 3010 in our example. The IHB records a liability for subsidiary 2100 and an asset for subsidiary 2300.
6	When the IHC end-of-day process is run, bank statements are sent to each of the subsidiaries. The bank statements hold the activity for the corresponding current accounts for the previous day, in the same way as if the payments had been executed at an external bank. The accounting entries made under company code 2300 are a debit to the IHC cash clearing account and a credit to the IHC balance G/L account. The accounting entries made under company code 2100 are a debit to the IHC bank balance G/L account and a credit to the IHC cash clearing account. In addition, the IC AR invoice is cleared under company code 2300.

Table 3.2: Intercompany payments processing steps

3.3   Centralized incoming payments process flow

The third core process delivered with SAP's IHC module is centralized incoming payments, also known as centralized receipts, receivables on behalf of, or ROBO payments. This process is initiated when an external party, typically a customer, makes payment to a bank account owned by the in-house bank. The in-house bank receives the payment, creates a payment order that credits the subsidiary's current account, then passes it along to the appropriate subsidiary in the internal bank statement.

Figure 3.7 shows what the payment structure would look like before centralizing incoming payments with an in-house bank.

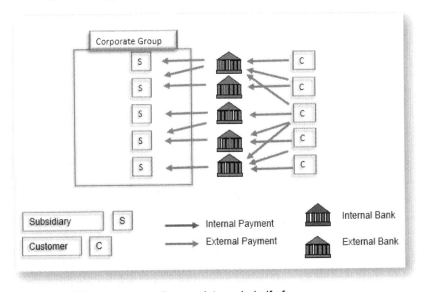

Figure 3.7: Before implementing receipts on behalf of

After implementing an in-house bank, receipts from customers across subsidiaries can be sent to an in-house bank's external bank account. Figure 3.8 shows a simplified example of how the payment structure for this company could change with an in-house bank.

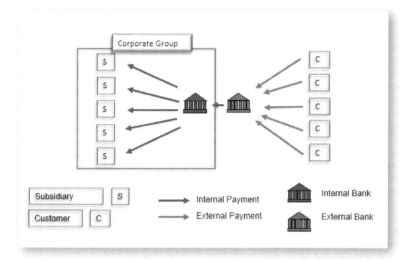

Figure 3.8: After implementing receipts on behalf of

Implementation hurdle

 Of the three core processes supported by SAP's IHC module, the centralized incoming payments process is the most difficult for most companies to implement. This is because, for the process to flow automatically, external customers must send specific reference information with their payment which is used by SAP to determine the correct current account/subsidiary the payment is for. Thus, the success rate of this process is dependent on external customers.

Table 3.3 outlines the steps involved in the centralized incoming payments process.

Step	Description
1	An external customer sends a payment to an external bank account associated with the IHB.
2	The payment is received in the bank statement from the IHB's external bank.
3	When the external bank statement is posted to the SAP general ledger, SAP debits the main G/L account for the external house bank account, and credits a cash clearing account for the external house bank account.
4	The IHB recognizes the incoming payment as belonging to subsidiary 2500, and so creates a payment order that credits the IHB current account for subsidiary 2500 and debits the IHB clearing partner account.
5	The in-house bank's end-of-day processing steps are run, during which an internal bank statement is sent from the in-house bank to each of the subsidiaries and contain activity processed at the in-house bank for that day. The in-house bank sends bank statements periodically (typically daily) to the subsidiaries that have accounts at the IHB. Within the next bank statement from the IHB to the subsidiary, the incoming payment is sent. A second action that occurs when the IHC end-of-day process is run is the posting of the day's IHC activity to the SAP general ledger of the company code where the IHB resides, which is company code 3010 in our example.
6	As the bank statement is posted in the subsidiary, it debits the main G/L account for the in-house bank account and credits a cash clearing account for the internal house bank account. This is posting area 1 of the bank statement postings. With posting area 2, the cash clearing account for the internal house bank account is debited and a credit is made to the customer account, if the customer can be determined, or to an IHC AR unapplied receipts clearing account.

Table 3.3: Centralized incoming payments processing steps

The steps in Table 3.3 are shown in the diagram in Figure 3.9.

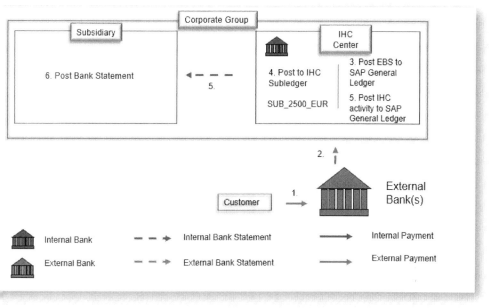

Figure 3.9: Process flow for centralized incoming payments

3.4 Manual payment orders

As mentioned earlier, SAP refers to payment orders created by running the AP payment program as "payment orders generated automatically", versus payment orders that are manually entered at the in-house bank as "payment orders generated manually". The reason for initiating a manual payment order may be that the subsidiary is not operational in SAP or, for one-off emergency, time-sensitive payments.

Manual payment orders can be either internal (intercompany) or external (generating an external payment), and they can be outgoing payments or direct debits/drawdowns. The process flow of manual payment orders is a subset of the process for payment orders generated automatically, such as payment on behalf of and centralized receipts.

The programs to enter manual payment orders can be found via following the menu path: Accounting • Financial Supply Chain Management • In-House Cash • Account Management • IHC Payment Orders • Create Payment Order • Bank Transfer or Debit Memo. The transaction codes for the four manual payment order programs are listed below:

- ▶ IHC1IP – Create Internal Payment Order – outgoing

- ▶ IHC1EP – Create External Payment Order – outgoing

- ▶ IHC1ID – Create Internal Payment Order – debit memo (incoming payment)

- ▶ IHC1ED – Create External Payment Order – debit memo (incoming payment)

Table 3.4 describes the steps in SAP when making an internal manual payment order. In our example, subsidiary 2300 sends a payment of 50,000 EUR to subsidiary 2100. This is a cashless intercompany payment to subsidiary 2300 through the in-house bank. Notice how the manual payment orders are a shortened version of the corresponding "payment orders generated automatically" process.

Step	Description
1	The in-house bank staff enters an internal payment order from the SUB_2300_EUR account to the SUB_2100_EUR account. Once the user executes the "Post" button, the system debits subsidiary 2300's current account and credits subsidiary 2100's current account in the amount of the payment.
2	The in-house bank's end-of-day process is run, during which an internal bank statement is sent from the in-house bank to each of the subsidiaries containing activity processed at the IHB for the day. A second action that occurs when the IHC end-of-day process is run is the posting of the day's IHC activity to the SAP general ledger of the company code where the IHB resides, which is company code 3010 in our example. The IHB records a liability for subsidiary 2300 and an asset for subsidiary 2100.

Step	Description
3	When the IHC end-of-day process is run, bank statements are sent to each of the subsidiaries. The bank statements hold the activity for the corresponding current accounts for the current day, in the same way as if the payments had been executed at an external bank. The accounting entries made under company code 2300 are a debit to the IHC cash clearing account and a credit to the IHC balance G/L account. The accounting entries made under company code 2100 are a debit to the IHC bank balance G/L account and a credit to the IHC cash clearing account. In addition, a credit is made to the intercompany customer account for 2100, with the use of the electronic bank statement search string configuration.

Table 3.4: Process steps for a manual internal payment order

Table 3.5 outlines the steps in SAP when making a manual external payment order. In our example, subsidiary 2300 sends a payment of 90,000 EUR to an external business partner.

Step	Description
1	The in-house bank receives a payment from subsidiary 2300, and creates a payment order that, when posted, debits the current account of subsidiary 2300 and creates a payment request that is a payment from the in-house bank to subsidiary 2300's external business partner.
2	The Treasury payment program is run for the IHC payments. The payment request created in Step 1 is cleared.
3	When the Treasury payment program is run for the IHC payments in Step 2, a payment file is generated and is sent to the bank. The payment file contains the payment to the subsidiary's vendor.
4	The external bank pays the vendor.
5	When the IHC end-of-day process is run, an internal bank statement is sent from the in-house bank to the subsidiary, and the current day's activity is posted to the SAP general ledger of the company code where the in-house bank resides, which is 3010 in our example. The internal bank statement holds the activity for the corresponding IHC current bank account for the previous day.

Step	Description
6	On the next business day, the in-house bank's external bank statement is processed in SAP under the in-house bank's company code, and it records the cleared payment sent on behalf of the in-house bank to subsidiary 2300's external business partner.

Table 3.5: Process steps for manual external payment orders

3.5 End-of-day processing

All payments processed through the IHC module run through the end-of-day processing steps described here. This is a mandatory process when using SAP's IHC module. There are a number of steps to finalize the IHC activity for a day, such as posting the balances of the IHC current accounts to the SAP general ledger, calculating interest and other fees, and creating and generating daily bank statements – all tasks that a real bank would do, which are included in the end-of-day process.

A company implementing SAP's IHC module sets a time of day when the IHB end-of-day activities start, and any payments received after that time roll into the next business day. Shortly after the cutoff time, the end-of-day processing steps are run. The end-of-day SAP programs are shown in Figure 3.10.

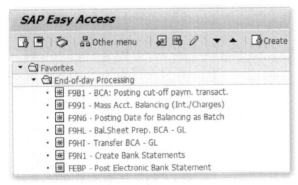

Figure 3.10: IHC end-of-day processing programs

The IHC end-of-day processing steps can be either scheduled or run manually. Most implementations schedule the IHC end-of-day process so it runs at the same time seven days a week. If there is no activity on weekend days, which would typically be the case, no postings are made. Table 3.6 describes the steps involved in the IHC end-of-day process in SAP.

Step	Description
F9B1	Move IHC date to next business date. This step closes the current date in In-House Cash and any other transactions entered into the system are processed by IHC on the next date.
F991	F996 for a single account. Use transaction code F991 to calculate interest (account balancing) across all internal accounts.
F9HL	Balance sheet preparation. This is a required preparatory step that is run to keep SAP current; no postings are made to the general ledger in this step.
F9HI	FI transfer. The IHC balances are posted to the general ledger in this step.
F9N1	Create and send bank statements from IHC. The in-house bank sends a bank statement to all participants who processed payments through IHC.
FEBP	Post internal bank statements to participants. The bank statements need to be posted to the general ledger for each of the participants; it offsets postings made during the AP payment program.

Table 3.6: IHC end-of-day processing steps

4 Master data related to IHC processing

This chapter covers the master data relevant to the IHC module, which is outlined in Table 4.1.

Master data	Description
Banks	The information required by financial institutions for payments, such as the SWIFT/BIC code, bank name, etc. is stored in the bank master data.
Business partners	The business partner (BP) is the holder/owner of the bank accounts at the IHB. The proper roles must be assigned to the business partner before it can be an IHC account owner. The two roles that must be assigned to the BP are the account holder and correspondence recipient.
Current accounts	Current accounts are bank accounts at an in-house bank. As with bank accounts at external banks, there can be different types of in-house bank current accounts. The current account holds all relevant information about the bank accounts. The current account master data holds the settings such as the currency of the account, the rate at which interest is charged on the account, any charges relevant to the account, etc. When displaying a current account master record, users are able to see the account balance, the transactions on the account, and a history of bank statements sent for the account.
Vendor master record	Both external and intercompany accounts payable invoices can be paid through the in-house bank. The fields in an accounts payable master record that are key to IHC processing are the payment method and bank details.
Customer master record	As with the accounts payable master record, the accounts receivable master record credit memos can be paid through the IHB. The fields in an accounts receivable master record that are key to IHC processing are the payment method and bank details.

Master data	Description
General ledger account	To support IHC processing, several new general ledger accounts need to be created.

Table 4.1: Types of master data relevant to IHC processing

Build a solid foundation

 It is critical to create a solid foundation for payment processing. Without a solid foundation and controlled processes, it is difficult to achieve efficient payment processing. Because SAP's IHC solution is a very integrated module, setting a solid foundation for payment processing involves an organization's Accounting, Treasury, Accounts Payable, and Accounts Receivable departments, as well as other key stakeholders.

4.1 Bank master data

Let us start with key master data. This is the bank master data stored in the bank master record table (BNKA). This master data is key to payment processing because it holds bank information that is used in all external payments from SAP. The information held in the bank master data is forwarded to the bank for payments sent from SAP.

In order to make payments from SAP, the bank master data holds required information about financial institutions, such as a financial institution's bank number, SWIFT/BIC code, bank name and more, which are stored in the BNKA.

Whenever a payment instruction is created based on incorrect bank data, bank repair fees can be charged by the bank to process those payments. This leads to higher costs and lower overall payment efficiency.

Important fields in the Bank Master data are listed below:

▶ Bank country – this field identifies the country of the bank.

▶ Bank key – an identifier of a bank in a country.

▶ Name and address of the bank: these fields describe the name of the bank and its address.

▶ SWIFT/BIC Code – the SWIFT code is a unique identification for financial institutions.

▶ Bank number – the 'Bank number' field is known by different names in different countries and the size of this field varies from country to country; e.g. in the US, the 'Bank number' field is known as the 'ABA number', and its length is 9 numeric characters.

Figure 4.1 shows a sample screenshot of bank master data.

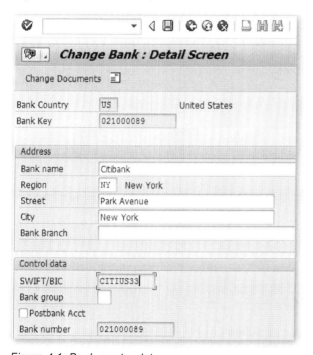

Figure 4.1: Bank master data

Due to its sensitive nature, many SAP customers have the bank master data "locked down" and managed exclusively by one department such as Treasury or Accounts Payable.

As an in-house bank is a bank within an organization, it requires a bank key in SAP, just as external banks have a defined bank key. This bank key is a required field when creating the bank area within the IHC configuration. Because this is a special type of bank key, it is created using the Create In-House Cash Center Bank program (transaction code FIHC), as opposed to Create Bank program (transaction code FI01). Figure 4.2 shows the definition of the bank key to be used for an IHC house bank. The information stored with the IHC bank key is the same as that stored with the bank keys representing external banks.

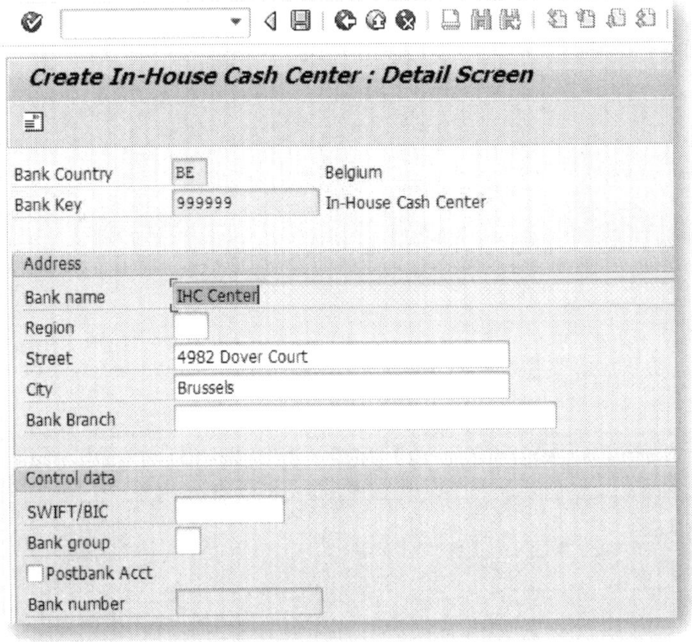

Figure 4.2: Definition of IHC bank key

4.2   Business partner master data

Business partners are a key component of the SAP In-House Cash module. In In-House Cash, business partners represent the participating legal entities, and are assigned to In-House Cash current accounts. An intercompany business partner must be set up for each entity participating in IHC processing.

Business partners are created or modified through transaction code BP. For the system to be user-friendly, it is important to keep the naming convention consistent. For example, entities that have intercompany loans could have associated business partners with the naming convention SUB_XXXX, where XXXX is the four-character company code number (e.g. SUB_1000). The business partner ID is 10 characters long.

When you assign a role to a business partner, you enable functionality that can be used for that business partner. All business partners that are owners of an IHC current account must have the Account Holder and Bank Statement Recipient roles assigned, in addition to the General Business Partner role, which SAP creates automatically. Below is an explanation of the functionality contained in each of these roles:

▶ ACCOUNT HOLDER (BKK010)
   The account holder role is applied to business partners holding accounts at the in-house bank. In-House Cash accounts are assigned to a company code, and are tied to a business partner. For all intercompany business partners, the trading partner field should be populated with the trading partner that represents the entity in SAP. The allowable validity date range for the BP role is confirmed when the role is assigned to the business partner. The validity date should correspond to the opening date of the associated current account.

▶ BANK STATEMENT RECIPIENT (BKK030)
   This role is assigned to any business partner that receives automatically generated account statements from In-House Cash. In general, this is assigned to every business partner that has an account holder role.

Business partner validity date

The validity date range of the BP role is validated when assigning the business partner as the account holder of a current account. Therefore, the validity date of the account holder role should correspond to the opening date of the account holder's current account.

If business partners have been created for other SAP modules, the use of the BP type is a way to categorize business partners based on their usage. For example, the business partners created for IHC processing could have a BP type SUTR (Treasury Subsidiary BP) so that users can distinguish them from business partners used in other SAP modules, such as the Credit Management module in the SAP system (see Figure 4.3).

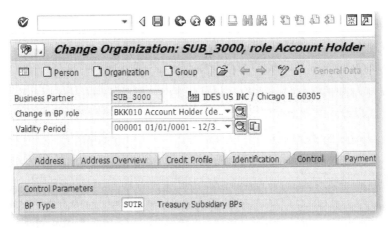

Figure 4.3: Business partner types functionality allow business partners to be categorized

The in-house bank activity is recorded in the financial statements of the in-house bank's assigned company code. The accounting entries related to in-house bank activities are excluded from the consolidated financial statements of a group of companies, which include the business units, using intercompany elimination transactions.

The bank accounts used for IHC processing are entered into the business partner master record on the PAYMENT TRANSACTIONS tab, as is done for vendors, as shown in Figure 4.4.

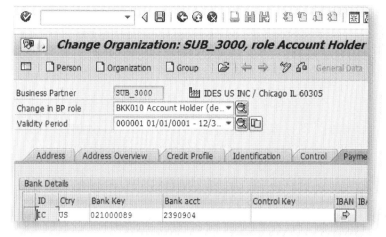

Figure 4.4: Bank account information in the intercompany business partner master record

Set validity date on role assignment

You need to set the validity date of the business partner's role assignment to be the same date as the opening date on the current accounts, otherwise you get an error message when creating the current accounts. To set the validity date on the role assignment to the business partner, select the Role Detail icon to the right of the role assignment. You then see a popup window, as shown in Figure 4.5. Set the date in the VLD FROM column for both roles. Save your changes.

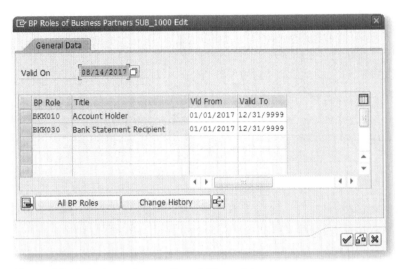

Figure 4.5: Set role assignment's valid from date

4.3   IHC current account master data

Current accounts are the bank accounts at the in-house bank. These accounts are also referred to as virtual accounts. All relevant information related to the IHC virtual accounts are stored in the account master data. Current accounts track all payments sent through the current accounts on behalf of their subsidiaries, as well as the current account balances. Business partners with an account holder role, as outlined previously, are assigned to current accounts.

Current accounts are mapped one-to-one to house bank accounts, which are not master data; this is important to mention because it is a relevant part of the design. Every in-house cash current account is created as a house bank account. This enables the in-house bank accounts to function in the same way as external bank accounts function in SAP for payment and bank statement processing.

Every subsidiary included in the IHC implementation should hold at least one account in the in-house bank. This account serves as a bank account that the IHC activity is routed through. Payments in a currency where the subsidiary does not have an IHC virtual account post to the virtual account in the entity's functional currency and are immediately converted to the virtual account currency using the exchange rate speci-fied in configuration.

The balance in these IHC current accounts shows the intercompany In-House Cash balance between each subsidiary and the in-house bank. Like an external bank account, bank statements containing all the trans-actions processed through the account are generated daily and delivered back to the account owner (the subsidiary) for posting and reconciliation. In this way, the IHC payments and SAP balances are captured in the SAP general ledger of each participating company code.

When current accounts are created, they are assigned a product and a bank area. The different products are defined in configuration. Table 4.2 outlines different types of current accounts needed for our example sce-nario.

Type of account	Product	Naming convention	Description
CPD	IHC-CPD	IHC-CPD	Creating this account is an SAP requirement.
SUB	IHC-SUB	SUB-CCCC-CUR	Similar to a bank account at an external bank, these are subsidi-ary bank accounts with the in-house bank. The standard IHC current accounts are used for all transactions processed through the in-house bank for the subsid-iary.
			Bank statements are generated and sent to the subsidiaries that have an account at the in-house bank, just as a bank would send bank statements to the owners of bank accounts.
			The naming convention used for this type of account is:
			SUB = subsidiary current ac-count
			CCCC = 4-digit company code

Type of account	Product	Naming convention	Description
EXT	IHC-EXT	EXT-CCCC-CUR	There is an IHC current account for each clearing partner held by the bank area owner and used for IHC payment processing. This account is used to record IHC activity executed between the in-house bank and the external bank accounts. The naming convention used for this type of account is: EXT = external current account CCCC = 4-digit company code. CUR = currency of the current account

Table 4.2: Types of IHC Accounts

The steps to create a current account are outlined in the following section.

To create an IHC current account, follow the menu path: ACCOUNTING • FINANCIAL SUPPLY CHAIN MANAGEMENT • IN-HOUSE CASH • ACCOUNT • CREATE, or go to transaction code F9K1. Figure 4.6 shows the input screen to F9K1.

Changing the opening date

Note: it is not possible to change the opening date of the IHC account after the account has been created.

Specify the bank area, account number, business partner, opening date of the account, and the product, which is the type of account. In addition, select the DEACTIVATE CHECK DIGIT indicator.

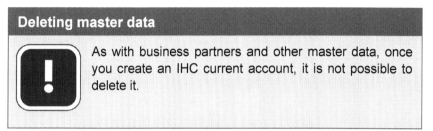

Deleting master data

As with business partners and other master data, once you create an IHC current account, it is not possible to delete it.

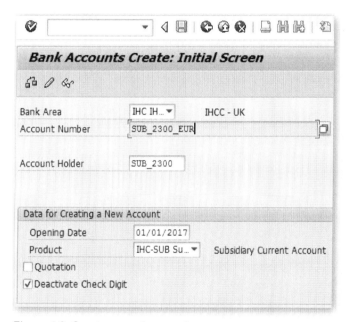

Figure 4.6: Create current account

▶ BASIC DATA tab

Figure 4.7 shows the BASIC DATA tab. The BASIC DATA tab contains the date the account was opened, the currency, the account holder and the current STATUS of the account.

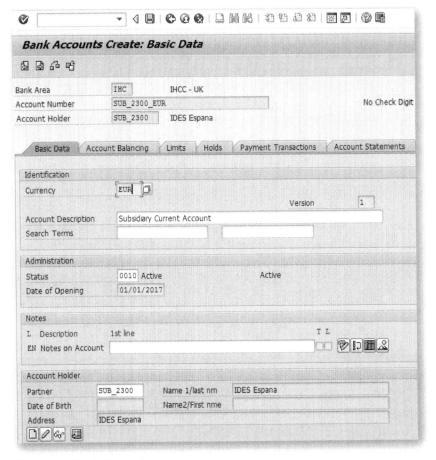

Figure 4.7: Basic Data tab

▶ ACCOUNT BALANCING tab

Conditions are set on the ACCOUNT BALANCING tab. The different conditions fall into three condition groups: interest, charges and value dates (see Figure 4.8). The CONDITION AREA determines the condition groups that can be assigned to the account. The interest condition group drives how interest is calculated on account balances as part of the account balancing process. The charges condition group determines the types of charges that apply to the account. The value date condition group is used to make adjustments to the value dates in specific IHC payments. The conditions linked to the condition areas are set in configuration.

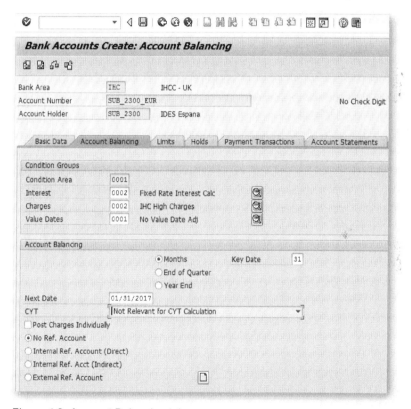

Figure 4.8: Account Balancing tab

▶ LIMITS tab

The LIMITS tab shows any withdrawal limits that may apply to the account, as shown in Figure 4.9.

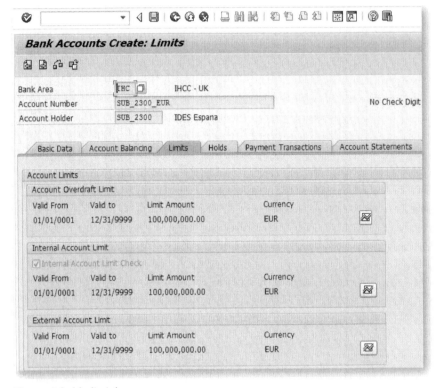

Figure 4.9: Limits tab

▶ ACCOUNT STATEMENTS tab

On the ACCOUNT STATEMENTS tab, enter the business partner corresponding to the account holder and subsidiary of the account, as shown in Figure 4.10. The frequency for generating bank statements are set on this tab, as well as the format of the bank statements. In our example scenario, the IHC bank statements are sent on a daily basis from the in-house bank as FINSTA IDocs. The Next Date field shows the date the account's next bank statement will be sent.

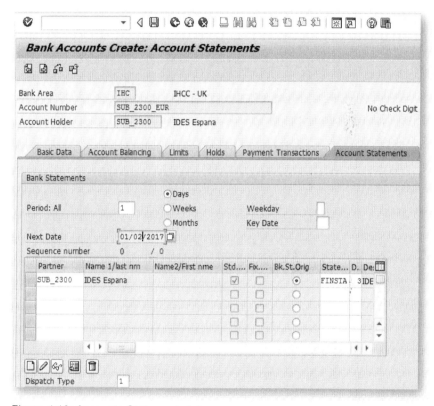

Figure 4.10: Accounts Statements tab

► CONTROL DATA tab

The General Ledger Group is specified on the CONTROL DATA tab, which drives how the current account is posted to the SAP General Ledger. This is shown in Figure 4.11.

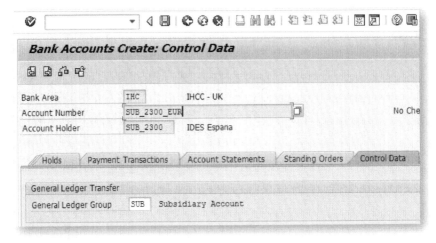

Figure 4.11: Control Data tab

► ADMINISTRATION DATA tab

The ADMINISTRATION DATA tab contains fields such as the internal account number for the account (this is how SAP tracks the current account), the calendar that is to be used for processing the account, and administrative information such as the user who created the account, on what date and at what time, as shown in Figure 4.12.

When the user presses the save icon, a message such as "Account SUB_2300_EUR has been created" is displayed.

At any time, users can select the ACCOUNT BALANCE or DISPLAY TURNO-VERS buttons to display the account balance or the payment transactions made through an IHC current account.

56

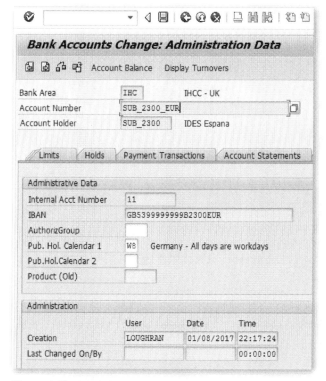

Figure 4.12: Administration Data tab

4.4 Accounts payable master data

The following fields in the vendor master record are relevant for In-House Cash processing:

1. An In-House Cash payment method must be assigned to a vendor. If there is more than one payment method maintained in a vendor master, the desired payment method must be explicitly specified for each invoice; otherwise, the payment method is determined by the timing of the different payment method payment runs.

2. In some cases, the payment method supplement is configured for special processing in In-House Cash.

3. 'Individual payment' indicator should typically not be set for any vendor. If this indicator is set for a vendor within a company code, then
all payments for that vendor from that company code are processed
individually, rather than bundled together.

4. The house bank field may be set to the IHB house bank ID.

5. Typically, only one set of PAYMENT TRANSACTIONS bank details
should be maintained in each vendor master record in order to reflect payment delivery instructions for that vendor. If more than one
set of details is maintained for a vendor, then the system automatically utilizes the first line of banking instructions for all invoice payments that are processed, unless the partner bank type identifier of
an alternative line of bank details from the master record is explicitly
entered into the partner bank type field in the AP invoice. Note that
for intercompany vendors that receive payment into their IHB accounts, the bank details should reflect the IHB bank key and current
account number.

Following good naming conventions

It is advisable to use a consistent naming convention for
the partner bank type (e.g. XEUR, XGBP, etc.) to provide clarity for the use of different bank detail lines in the
master record.

4.5 Customer receivable master data

As with the accounts payable master record, account receivable master
record debit memos can be paid through the IHB. The relevant fields in
an accounts payable master record are also relevant to the accounts
receivable master record.

4.6 General ledger master data

To support IHC processing, several new general ledger accounts need to
be created. The new accounts support the In-House Cash postings to
the ledger. These general ledger accounts need to be created under the

company code the IHB is assigned to. In addition, because a new (internal) house bank account is created under the subsidiaries who route payments through the in-house bank, cash-related general ledger accounts need to be created in the subsidiary company codes. Table 4.3 shows the list of accounts that are required for IHC processing. All the accounts are balance sheet accounts.

Account name	Where	Account description
IHC EOD technical clearing	In-house bank company code	One of two technical clearing accounts required for IHC daily end-of-day processing, which posts the daily IHC subledger activity to the general ledger of the company code that owns the IHC process. This account is zero at end of every day.
		You post to this account for all IHC postings when the end-of-day process is run. The postings to this G/L account can be in any currency.
		In our example, 113009 is used for this G/L account.
IHC EOD summary clearing	In-house bank company code	One of two technical clearing accounts required for IHC daily end-of-day processing, which posts the daily IHC subledger activity to the general ledger of the company code that owns the IHC process. This account is zero at end of every day.
		You post to this account for all IHC postings when the end-of-day process is run.
		G/L account 113111 is used in our example.
IHC external payment clearing	In-house bank company code	Account used for IHC external payment processing. It is the offset to Cash-In-Transit used by the Treasury Payment Program (F111) for IHC Payments. This is not used for posting intercompany IHC entries to the general ledger.
		G/L account 113110 is used in our example.

Account name	Where	Account description
IHC I/C balance	All company code(s)	This account is the G/L reflection of the I/C balance that exists as a result of the activity processed through IHC. The balance is equal to the IHC virtual account balance. Trading partner field should be populated in entries to this account. At the IHB, you post to this G/L account as part of the end-of-day process. At the subsidiary level, this G/L account is posted to by the bank statements (internal or external). G/L account 119000 is used in our example. (This account is put in the IHC payables/receivables configuration for the SUB current accounts.)
IHC I/C balance '0' and IHC house bank Clearing '1' accounts	Subsidiary company codes	The IHC house bank accounts in the subsidiary company codes require a '0' account and at least one cash clearing account, which is referred to as the '1' account. The '1' account is a payments-in-transit suspense account for AP payments executed by the AP Payment Program (F110) and sent to the in-house bank. The open items in the '1' account are cleared when the IHC bank statement posts. In our example, accounts 119000 and 119001 are used for these G/L account.
IHC AR unapplied receipts clearing	Subsidiary company codes	Suspense (clearing) account used as part of the cash application process for IHC I/C AR receipts processing. In our example, G/L account 119005 is used to track unapplied receipts.
Payment request clearing account	In-house bank company code	G/L account used to track the external IHC payments. The payment request clearing account is 100999 in our example.

Table 4.3: General ledger accounts needed for IHC processing

The IHC house bank accounts defined in the subsidiary company codes and the external bank accounts used at the in-house bank require a main bank G/L account and at least one cash clearing account. The cash clearing accounts hold payments in transit; e.g. payments that have not yet cleared the bank.

Segregation of incoming versus outgoing IHC payments

 It may be helpful to create a separate incoming payments temporary suspense (clearing) account for IHC I/C AR receipts processing to separate the outgoing from the incoming IHC payments, if collections on behalf of is implemented.

The trading partner field is automatically populated by SAP in the relevant IHC postings, assuming the business partners have been defined with the trading partner field populated.

5 Application side IHC processing

Now that we have covered the relevant background information, as well as the IHC required master data, let's have a detailed look at the process flow for each of the five processes mentioned in Chapter 3.

5.1 In-House Cash processes

Below are the five IHC processes that are covered in detail in this chapter:

▶ payments on behalf of

▶ intercompany payments

▶ centralized incoming payments

▶ manual payment orders

▶ end-of-day processing

5.2 Payments on behalf of

The payments on behalf of example we are using here is a vendor payment for company code 2100 which is made through the in-house bank. Company code 2100 makes an IHC payment. Once the in-house bank receives the payment, the Treasury payment program is executed to pay company code 2100's vendor. The payment is made by domestic wire transfer.

The payments on behalf of process flow diagram from Figure 3.3 is repeated here in Figure 5.1 for convenience.

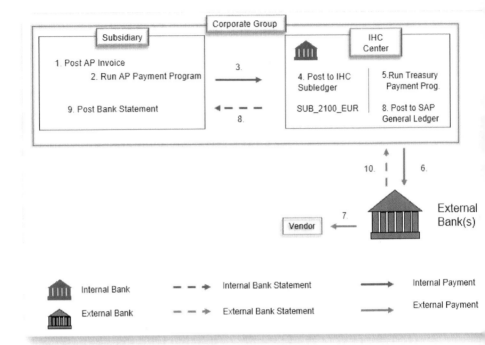

Figure 5.1: Payments on behalf of process flow

Before getting started, we can see in Figure 5.2 that the in-house bank has been added as a house bank account under company code 2100. House bank accounts can be viewed by executing transaction code FI12. SAP's IHC solution is completely integrated with the existing AP and AR processes.

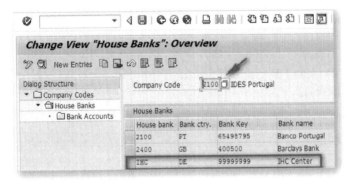

Figure 5.2: View IHC house bank under company code 2100

Drilling down into the house bank account from Figure 5.2, we see the BANK KEY and BANK ACCOUNT NUMBER for the in-house bank account, which is company code 2100's current account number at the in-house bank (see Figure 5.3).

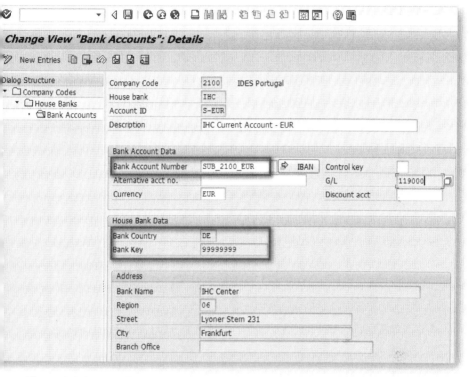

Figure 5.3: View IHC house bank account under company code 2100

The last task we run before starting the payments on behalf of example is to validate the account balance in the SUB_2100_EUR current account at the in-house bank. We do this by executing the Balance List by Key Date (Value Date or Posting Date) program by following the menu path: ACCOUNTING • FINANCIAL SUPPLY CHAIN MANAGEMENT • IN-HOUSE CASH • INFORMATION SYSTEM • BALANCE LIST BY KEY DATE or by executing transaction code F970_VAL. This program shows the current balance amount in the IHC current accounts, as shown in Figure 5.4.

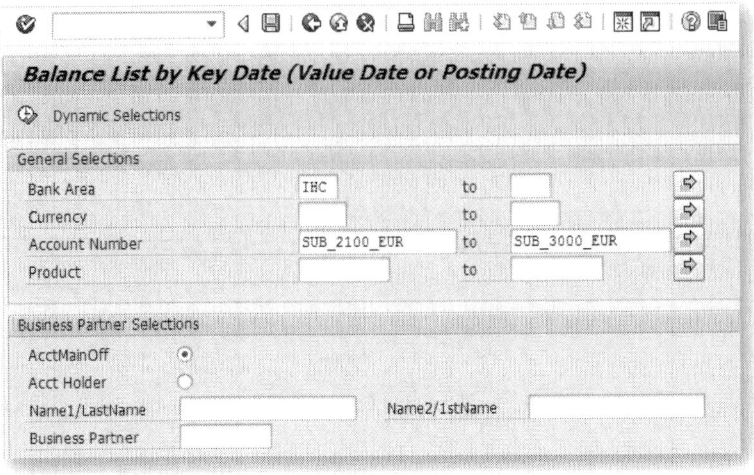

Figure 5.4: View IHC current account balances by key date

Figure 5.5 shows the output screen after executing transaction code F970_VAL. We can see that the balance in the SUB_2100_EUR account before starting the payment on behalf of example is zero.

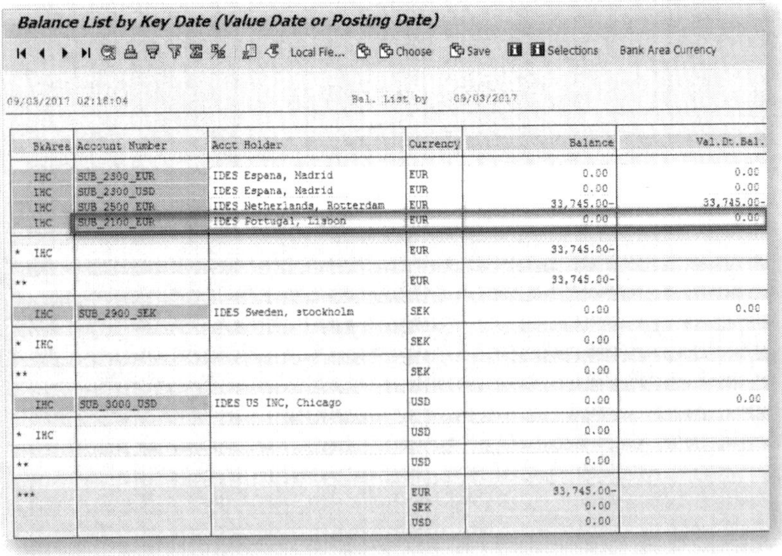

Figure 5.5: View IHC current account balances

We will now walk through the steps of the payments on behalf of process (outlined in Section 3.1) in detail:

Step 1: In the first step, the subsidiary enters the vendor invoice into SAP by following the SAP menu path: Accounting • Financial Accounting • Accounts Payable • Document Entry • Invoice or by executing transaction code FB60, as shown in Figure 5.6. The payment method in the invoice or in the vendor master should be an IHC-enabled payment method. In our example scenario, we use payment method J, which is the IHC external payment method.

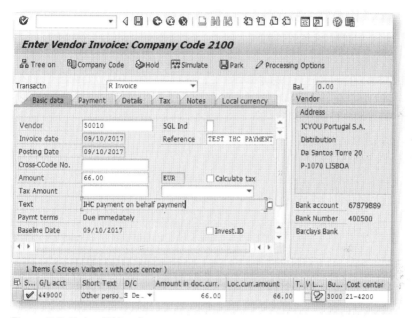

Figure 5.6: Enter AP invoice

Notice on the Payment tab that the IHC external payment method J is entered into the invoice, as shown in Figure 5.7.

Payment method supplement

SAP's IHC module supports the use of the payment method supplement field, in addition to the payment method, to determine how the payment should be paid by the in-house bank.

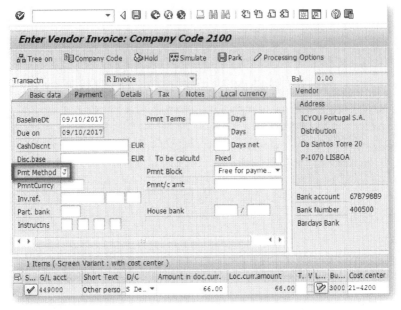

Figure 5.7: IHC external payment method entered in invoice

IHC AP payment method

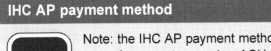

Note: the IHC AP payment method does not indicate the type of payment; e.g. wire, ACH, check. It simply indicates that the payment should be routed through the in-house bank. In this example, it is the in-house bank that determines how the vendor is to be paid.

After pressing the SAVE icon, the message in Figure 5.8: Document number for AP invoice is displayed to the user.

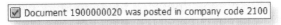

Figure 5.8: Document number for AP invoice

Step 2: In the next step, subsidiary 2100 initiates the AP payment program, which can be found by following the menu path: ACCOUNTING • FINANCIAL ACCOUNTING • ACCOUNTS PAYABLE • PERIODIC PROCESSING • PAYMENTS, or by executing transaction code F110. When the AP payment program is run, it clears the AP invoice and makes a credit entry to the IHC clearing account. See Chapter 6 for more information on the IHC accounting entries.

There are roughly four steps to running the AP payment program. The first step is to enter the parameters, which entails specifying the payments you want to pay. After entering the parameters, you execute the proposal run. In the proposal run, the SAP system informs you which invoices, based on the parameters entered, are to be paid. In the third, and typically final step, both the accounting entries are made to the SAP general ledger, and the payment medium is created. (These final two steps can be made separately or together.) In the case of IHC, the payment medium is a PAYEXT IDoc, which is sent to the in-house bank. Table 5.1 shows the steps involved in running the AP payment program.

Step	Description
Enter parameters	Users tell the SAP system what they want to pay.
Proposal run	The SAP system tells the user what payments will be made based on the parameters entered.
Payment run	Postings for the payment are made to the SAP General Ledger.
Create payment medium	Creates a PAYEXT payment IDoc that is sent to the in-house bank

Table 5.1: Steps to running the AP payment program

In the AP payment program, enter the current date in the Run Date field, and a unique identifier for the payment run in the Identification field, as shown in Figure 5.9.

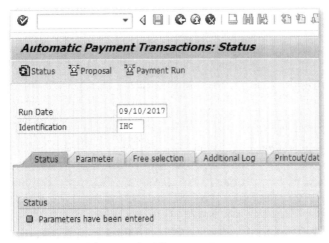

Figure 5.9: Initial screen to AP payment program

Next, enter the parameters; this is done by clicking the Parameters button, which takes the user to the screen shown in Figure 5.10. The date entered in the Posting Date field drives the posting date of the FI document created by the payment program. The next payment run date should be set to the date when the AP payment program will be run next. This information drives the payments picked up by the payment run; any payment that is due before the next payment run date is included. Enter the company code and the IHC payment method, as shown in Figure 5.10.

Press the PRINTOUT/DATA MEDIUM tab and enter the variant created on RFFOEDI1, as shown in Figure 5.11. This triggers the PAYEXT IDoc to be created when the payment medium is set up for this payment run. Press the SAVE icon to save the parameters entered. (For information on creating this variant, please see Section 7.3.4.)

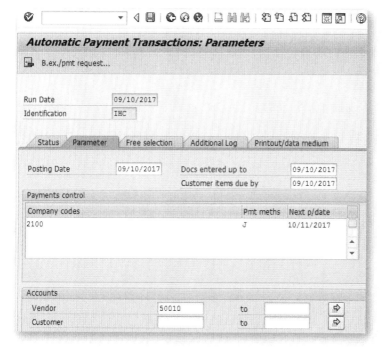

Figure 5.10: Enter AP payment program parameters

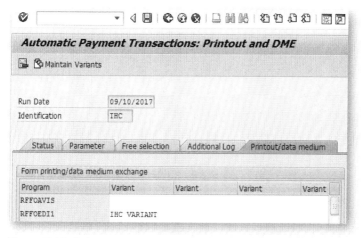

Figure 5.11: Select payment medium variant

The user is taken to the screen in Figure 5.12 that includes a message in the Status section indicating that the parameters for the payment run have been entered.

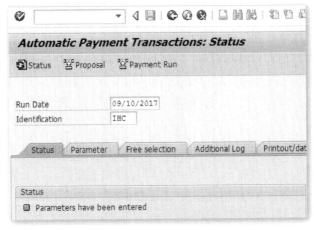

Figure 5.12: AP payment program parameters entered

The next step is the proposal run. The proposal run tells you what payments will be paid based on the parameters entered. To start the proposal run, click the Proposal button, as shown in Figure 5.12, which triggers a pop-up screen (Figure 5.13) in which you can either select to start the proposal run immediately or schedule a later time for it to run.

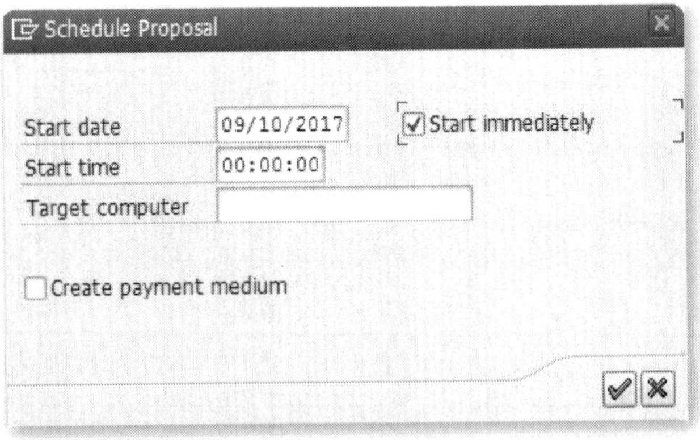

Figure 5.13: Schedule proposal popup message

After the proposal run is complete, the message "Payment proposal has been created" is displayed in the Status section of the next screen (see Figure 5.14).

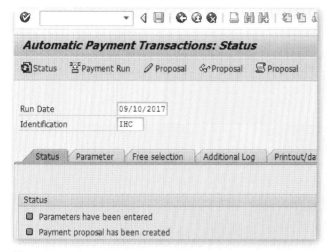

Figure 5.14: The payment proposal has been created

The user should evaluate the proposal run by clicking the Proposal button or by selecting EDIT • PROPOSAL • PROPOSAL LIST from the drop-down menu. In the List Variant pop-up screen that the system displays (not shown), press the Enter key on your keyboard. The system then displays the Payment List report, as shown in Figure 5.15.

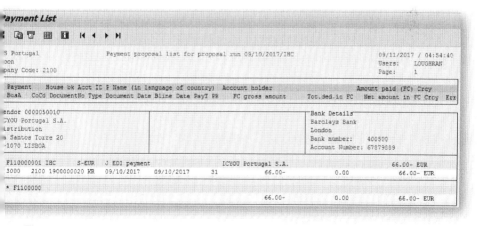

Figure 5.15: Proposal list report

The business user should validate the details of the payment and then click the back icon (the green arrow) to go back one screen when complete.

The last step is to execute the payment run by clicking the PAYMENT RUN button, as shown in the screen in Figure 5.14. The payment run makes the postings to the SAP General Ledger for the payment(s), and can also create the relevant payment medium.

After you click the PAYMENT RUN button, the system displays a pop-up screen (see Figure 5.16). As with the pop-up screen displayed in Figure 5.13 for the proposal run, you either select to start the payment run immediately or schedule when it should be carried out. In most cases, the payment run takes place immediately. For the payment run, there is an option to create the payment medium. This indicator should be selected so that a payment IDoc is sent to the in-house bank.

Figure 5.16: Schedule payment run and create payment medium

When the payment run is completed, a message is displayed to indicate this, as shown in Figure 5.17. The payment has been made from AP. The AP invoice is cleared. A PAYEXT IDoc has been sent to the in-house bank, and a payment order has been created.

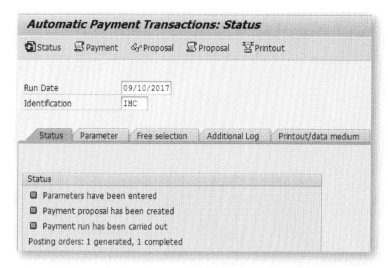

Figure 5.17: Payment run has completed successfully

To view the payment log, press the PAYMENT log button in Figure 5.17. The log shows the accounting entries made and that an IDoc will be created for this payment (see Figure 5.18).

```
04:55:58 Log for payment run for payment on 09/10/2017, identification IHC
04:55:58 >
04:55:58 > Additional log for vendor 50010 company code 2100
04:55:58 >
04:55:58 >          Posting documents additional log
04:55:58 > Currencies in line 1: EUR / EUR  Currencies in line 2: EUR / USD
04:55:58 > Document 2000000026 company code 2100 currency EUR payment method J
04:55:58 > LIt PK Acct          RA          Amount          Tax
04:55:58 >
04:55:58 > 001 25 0000050010                66.00           0.00
04:55:58 >                                  66.00           0.00
04:55:58 > 002 50 0000119001                66.00           0.00
04:55:58 >                                  66.00           0.00
04:55:58 >
04:55:58
04:55:58          payments by EDI / IDoc generation
04:55:58 IDOcs were generated for the following entries
04:55:58   Company code 2100    House bank IHC  Payment method J
```

Figure 5.18: AP payment run log

Step 3: The final step in running the AP payment program is to send a payment from the subsidiary to the in-house bank. The form of the payment sent is an SAP payment IDoc. The configuration for payment method J is what triggers SAP to route this payment through the in-house bank.

To view the payment IDoc created, execute transaction code WE02 and press execute. Note that business users do not view the contents of IDocs in a productive system. The internal SAP support user can see a screen similar to the one in Figure 5.19 that shows a PAYEXT IDoc being sent from the subsidiary (in the OUTBOUND IDOCS folder) to the in-house bank (in the INBOUND IDOCS folder).

Figure 5.19: Payment IDocs from subsidiary to IHB

By drilling down into either the outbound or inbound PAYEXT IDocs, the user can see that all the information related to the payment is sent from the subsidiary to the in-house bank (see Figure 5.20, which shows the AP payment run information). Each IDoc segment contains information on the payment being sent to the in-house bank. All relevant information on the payment is passed in the IDoc. To view the layout of the IDoc, go to Documentation in the IDoc Types program (transaction code WE60).

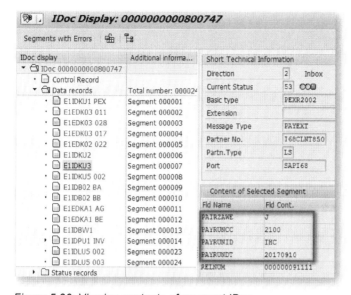

Figure 5.20: Viewing contents of payment IDoc

Step 4: In this step, the in-house bank receives the payment from subsidiary 2100. A payment order is created that, when posted, debits the current account of subsidiary 2100 and creates a payment request that is a payment from the in-house bank to subsidiary 2100's external vendor. When the payment order is initially created, it is created with a status of FLAGGED FOR POSTING. This status is comparable to a parked FI document. The payment order can be viewed by following the menu path: ACCOUNTING • FINANCIAL SUPPLY CHAIN MANAGEMENT • IN-HOUSE CASH • ACCOUNT MANAGEMENT • IHC PAYMENT ORDERS • PAYMENT ORDER BROWSER, or by executing transaction code IHC0 (see Figure 5.21).

Browser for IHC Payment Orders

⊕ Select IHC Payment Orders ⌄	💾 Save Variant ⌄	🗒		
Selection Criteria				
Selection Fld		Value From		Value To
Bank Area	=	IHC		
Payment Order				
Year				
Date Executed		9/10/2017		

Figure 5.21: Inputs to IHC payment order browser

The user must narrow down the search criteria; for example, by entering a BANK AREA and the DATE EXECUTED, and then pressing the ⊕ Select IHC Payment Orders icon. A screen similar to the one in Figure 5.22 is displayed.

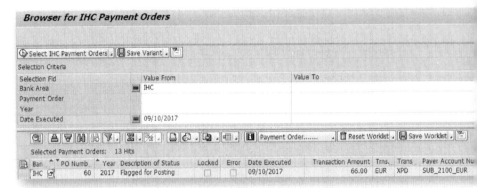

Figure 5.22: Executed IHC payment order browser

Because we are filtering by the value date, only one payment order is displayed. Note that its status is FLAGGED FOR POSTING. The display layout can be changed to show other fields by changing the default variant.

To finally post the payment order, select the payment order, right-click, and then select POST from the popup menu, as shown in Figure 5.23. Note: posting the payment order in this step does not make postings to the SAP general ledger. The IHC module has a subledger and its balances are posted to the SAP general ledger as part of the end-of-day process.

SAP displays an informational pop-up message similar to the one shown in Figure 5.24. This is one of the messages from SAP when posting a payment order. Here, it indicates the payment order has been successfully posted. The status on the payment order is now FINALLY POSTED. Press the Enter key to move past the pop-up messages.

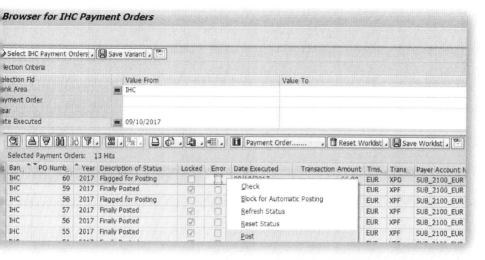

Figure 5.23: Select and right-click on the payment order to post it

Figure 5.24: Information message that payment order has been finally posted

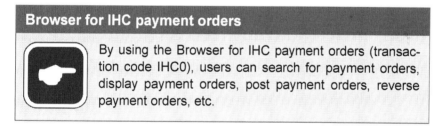

Browser for IHC payment orders

By using the Browser for IHC payment orders (transaction code IHC0), users can search for payment orders, display payment orders, post payment orders, reverse payment orders, etc.

At this point, the IHC current accounts are updated in the IHC subledger, an external payment method is determined from the IHC configuration, and a payment request is created to pay the external vendor from an IHC external bank account using the Treasury payment program. If there were multiple company codes paying this external vendor, the payments would be netted by the Treasury payment program and one payment would be sent to the vendor (as opposed to one payment for each company code if not using IHC).

SAP customers can choose to have the payment orders post automatically as opposed to manually posting the payment orders by scheduling the IHC post payment orders program. Also note that the payment orders can be posted all at once (as opposed to one at a time) by dragging and selecting multiple payment orders, then right-clicking on POST.

At any time, the users can drill down on the payment order from IHC0 to see all the details related to the payment orders. Figure 5.25 shows the OVERVIEW tab after drilling down on the payment order.

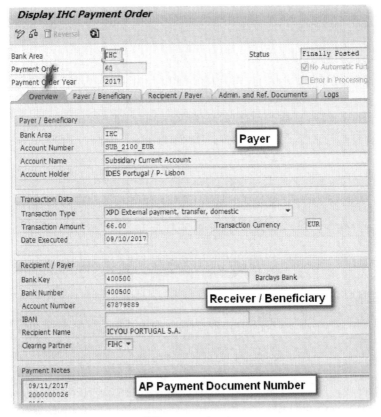

Figure 5.25: Drilldown on IHC payment order

The PAYER / BENEFICIARY tab shows the initiator of the payment order, as shown in Figure 5.26.

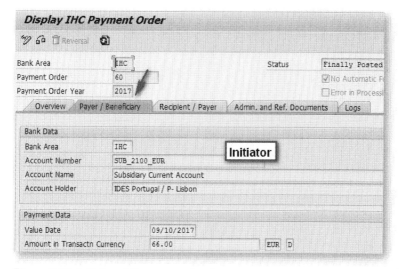

Figure 5.26: Initiator of the payment order

The RECIPIENT / PAYER tab shows the recipient or counterparty of the payment order, as shown in Figure 5.27.

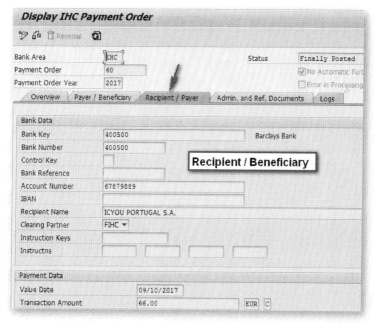

Figure 5.27: Recipient or counterparty of the payment order

On the ADMIN. AND REF. DOCUMENTS tab (after pressing the Refresh icon
) you see the payment request associated with this payment order, as
shown in Figure 5.28.

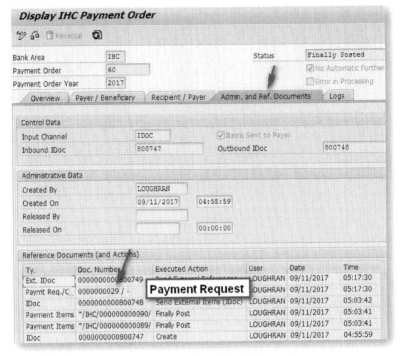

Figure 5.28: Administrative data and audit trail information

In the LOGS tab, SAP shows a short audit trail of the payment order, as
shown in Figure 5.29.

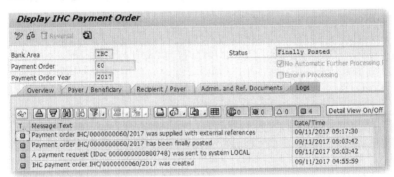

Figure 5.29: Processing log information on payment order

By pressing the [Detail View On/Off] button, SAP shows a detailed log/audit trail for the payment order (see Figure 5.30). This is extremely helpful if there are any issues that need to be resolved.

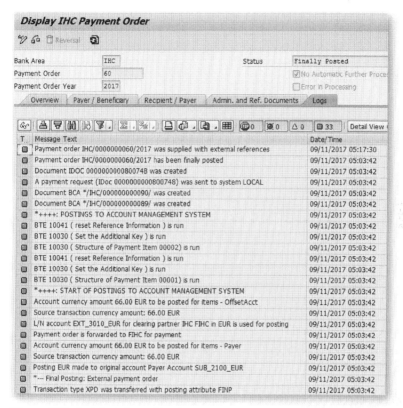

Figure 5.30: Detailed view of log for a payment order

Step 5: The Treasury payment program is run to execute the IHC payments. The payment request created in Step 4 is cleared in this step.

A payment request was automatically created with the posting of the payment order in Step 4. To view the payment request created, follow the menu path: FINANCIAL ACCOUNTING • BANKS • OUTGOINGS • AUTOMATIC PAYMENT • PAYMENT REQUESTS or execute transaction code F8BT to get to the Display Payment Requests program (see Figure 5.31). The IHC payments are paid from company code 3010 (i.e. the company code under which the in-house bank resides).

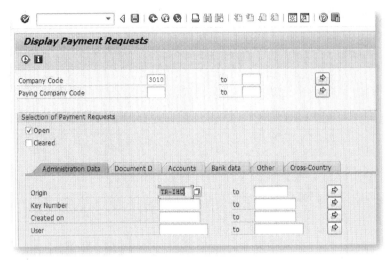

Figure 5.31: Display payment requests report

The user can filter on other fields such as the ORIGIN field to see only IHC-related payment requests. After entering the inputs to filter on the payment requests, the user should press the execute icon ⊕ to view the payment requests. Figure 5.32 shows the output display. The key number is a unique identifier for the payment. The key number goes across company codes.

Display Payment Requests

|◄ ◄ ► ►| 🔍 ☰ ▽ ⇕ 🔳 🖫 🖫 Choose 🖫 Save ∎

09/11/2017 05:26:44   Display Payment Requests

Key number	CoCd	DocumentNo	Year	Currency	Pymt curr.amnt	Partner	Origin	House bk	Acct ID	Methods
29	3010			EUR	66.00-	113110	TR-IHC	CITGB	EU845	1

Figure 5.32: Display payment requests output screen

Reporting on historical payments

The Display Payment Requests program can be used to view historical payments by selecting the Cleared indicator and deselecting the Open indicator. The user can drill down on the payment request to see all information related to the payment, as shown in Figure 5.33.

Detail: Display

09/03/2017 21:32:57 Detail: Display

Column	Contents
Key number	26
Paying company code	3010
Sending company code	3010
Company Code	3010
User Name	LOUGHRAN
Entry Date	09/03/2017
Local Currency	EUR
Invoice currency	EUR
Local currency 2	EUR
Local currency 3	USD
Payment currency	EUR
Amt.in loc.cur.	9,000.00-
LC2 amount	9,000.00-
LC3 amount	10,096.11-
Amount	9,000.00-
Local currency amount	9,000.00-
Payment currency amount	9,000.00-
Debit/Credit ind	H
Account type	S
Business partner	113110
G/L Account	113110
Name 1	ICYOU PORTUGAL S.A.
Name 2	DISTRIBUTION
Postal Code	1070
City	LISBOA
Street	DA SANTOS TORRE 20
Country Key	PT
Region	31
Name of the payee	ICYOU PORTUGAL S.A.
Name of the payee	DISTRIBUTION
Payee postal code	1070
City	LISBOA

Figure 5.33: Drilldown on payment request

The steps to run the Treasury payment program are the same four steps outlined for the AP payment program. As the steps were already outlined in detail for the AP payment program, we will not cover the steps for the Treasury payment program in the same detail. They are listed in Table 5.2.

Step	Description
Enter parameters	Users tell the SAP system what they want to pay.
Proposal run	The SAP system tells the user what payments will be made based on the parameters entered.
Payment run	Postings for the payment are made to the SAP general ledger.
Create payment medium	Creates a payment file that is sent to the bank.

Table 5.2: Treasury payment program steps

Figure 5.34 shows the completed payment run for the payment request created in this example.

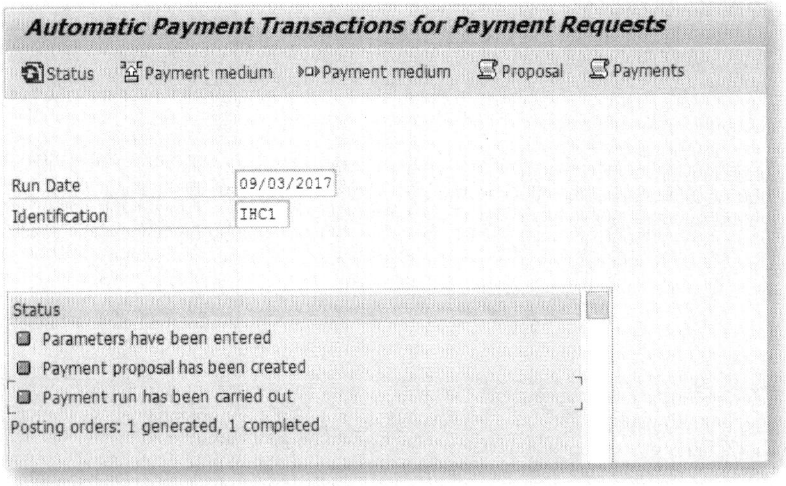

Automatic Payment Transactions for Payment Requests

Status Payment medium Payment medium Proposal Payments

Run Date   09/03/2017
Identification   IHC1

Status
- Parameters have been entered
- Payment proposal has been created
- Payment run has been carried out
Posting orders: 1 generated, 1 completed

Figure 5.34: Completed Treasury payment program run

The accounting entries made when the IHB executes the Treasury payment program can be seen in the payment log by pressing the ☐ Payments button (see Figure 5.35).

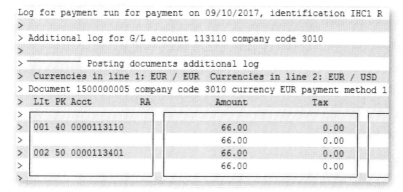

Figure 5.35: Treasury payment program log

Step 6: When the Treasury payment program is run for the IHC payments in Step 5, a payment file is generated and is sent to the bank. The
payment file contains the payment instructions to pay the external vendor. From F111, follow the menu path: ENVIRONMENT • PAYMENT MEDIUM •
DME ADMINISTRATION to view the payment file.

Figure 5.36: Display payment medium screen

Select the row displayed in Figure 5.36, and press the Display icon 🔍 to
view the payment file (see Figure 5.37). This payment file is sent to the
bank, which then transfers funds to the vendor.

Data Medium Overview

```xml
<?xml version="1.0" encoding="UTF-8"?>
<Document xsi:schemaLocation="urn:iso:std:iso:20022:tec
xmlns:xsi="http://www.w3.org/2001/XMLSchema-insta
  <CstmrCdtTrfInitn>
    <GrpHdr>
        <MsgId>1000031207</MsgId>
        <CreDtTm>2017-09-11T05:30:48</CreDtTm>
        <NbOfTxs>1</NbOfTxs>
        <CtrlSum>66.00</CtrlSum>
      <InitgPty>
          <Nm>IDES AG</Nm>
      </InitgPty>
    </GrpHdr>
    <PmtInf>
        <PmtInfId>1000031207</PmtInfId>
        <PmtMtd>TRF</PmtMtd>
        <BtchBookg>00000</BtchBookg>
        <NbOfTxs>1</NbOfTxs>
        <CtrlSum>66.00</CtrlSum>
      <PmtTpInf>
        <SvcLvl>
            <Cd>SEPA</Cd>
        </SvcLvl>
      </PmtTpInf>
        <ReqdExctnDt>2017-09-10</ReqdExctnDt>
      <Dbtr>
          <Nm>Euro Subsidiary - Belgium</Nm>
        <PstlAdr>
            <Ctry>BE</Ctry>
            <AdrLine>Brussels</AdrLine>
```

Figure 5.37: Payment file that is sent to the bank

Step 7: The external bank pays the vendor. This step is executed at the external bank.

Step 8: When the IHC end-of-day process is run, an internal bank statement is sent from the in-house bank to the subsidiaries that hold an account at the in-house bank, and the current day's activity is posted to the SAP general ledger of the company code where the in-house bank resides. For details of the full end-of-day processing steps, see Section 5.6. Only the specific steps relevant to this process are shown here.

The internal bank statement holds the activity for the corresponding IHC current bank accounts for the previous day. To initiate the process to send the internal bank statements, follow the menu path: ACCOUNTING • FINANCIAL SUPPLY CHAIN MANAGEMENT • IN-HOUSE CASH • PERIODIC PRO-CESSING • BANK STATEMENT • NEW RUN • MASS RUN, or execute transac-tion code F9N1 (see Figure 5.38).

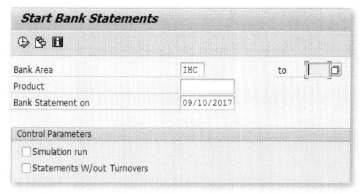

Figure 5.38: Input screen for mass run of internal bank statements

The transaction code F9N1 sends an internal bank statement for all current accounts at the in-house bank. After F9N1 is executed, the message in Figure 5.39 is displayed.

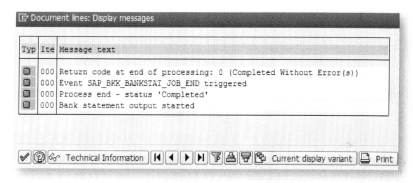

Figure 5.39: Message after executing F9N1 successfully

It is also possible to send bank statements for an individual IHC account using transaction code F9N7. F9N1 is the 'mass send' bank statements transaction, which sends a bank statement for all current accounts in selected bank area(s).

The IHC bank statements are sent as FINSTA IDocs. To view the FINSTA IDocs generated, follow the menu path: TOOLS • ALE • ALE ADMINISTRATION • MONITORING • IDOC DISPLAY • DISPLAY, or execute transaction code WE02. Figure 5.40 displays the bank statements sent for subsidiary 2100's current account. Note that business users do not view the contents of IDocs in a productive system.

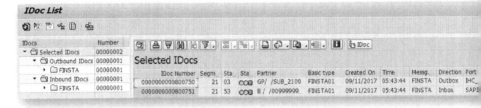

Figure 5.40: Internal FINSTA IDoc bank statements created

The outbound IDoc is from the in-house bank, and the inbound IDoc is to the SUB_2100's partner profile, as can be seen by viewing the control record of the inbound FINSTA IDoc (see Figure 5.41). (All IDocs have a control record that contains general information such as the sender and recipient related to the IDoc.)

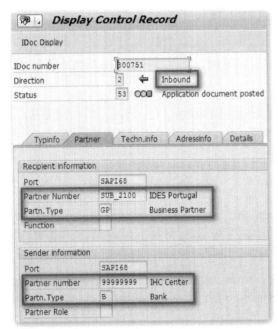

Figure 5.41: Control record of inbound FINSTA IDoc

Business users do not look at the IDoc contents, but SAP support might. Figure 5.42 shows the amount segment in the inbound IDoc.

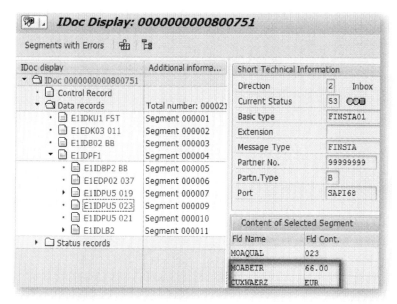

Figure 5.42: Bank statement transaction amount information

The internal bank statements are then posted by following the menu path: ACCOUNTING • FINANCIAL ACCOUNTING • BANKS • INPUT • BANK STATEMENT • POST, or by executing transaction code FEBP (see Figure 5.43).

Figure 5.44 shows the posting made for the payment on behalf of transaction made from company code 2100. When the transaction clears at the in-house bank, the posting debits the IHC House Bank Clearing account (2100/119001) and credits the IHC I/C Balance account (2100/119000). These are the same postings that would be made when an external bank statement is imported for an outgoing payment that has cleared the bank.

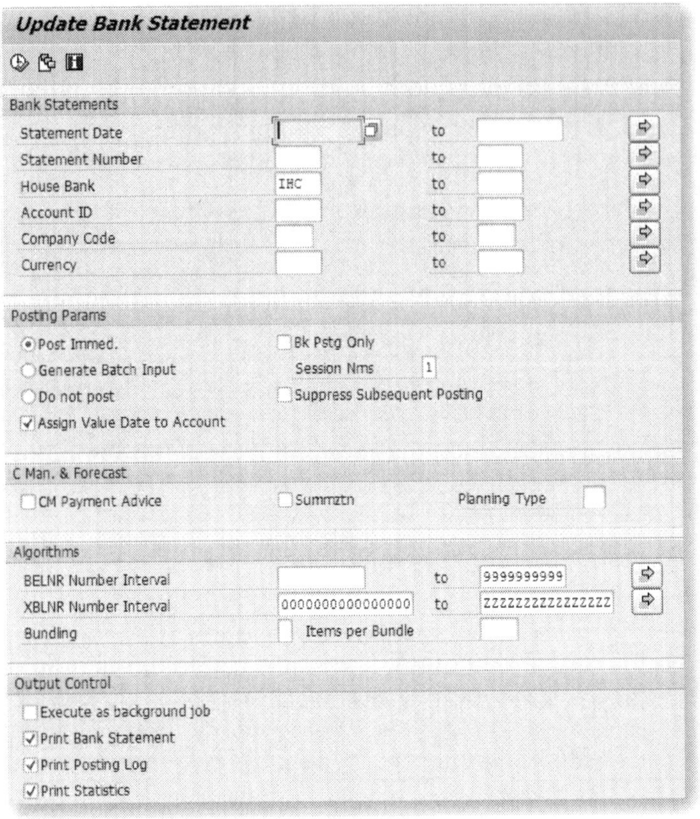
Update Bank Statement
Bank Statements
Statement Date
to
Statement Number
to
House Bank
IHC
to
Account ID
to
Company Code
to
Currency
to
Posting Params
◉ Post Immed.
○ Generate Batch Input
○ Do not post
☑ Assign Value Date to Account
☐ Bk Pstg Only
Session Nms
1
☐ Suppress Subsequent Posting
C Man. & Forecast
☐ CM Payment Advice
☐ Summztn
Planning Type
Algorithms
BELNR Number Interval
to
9999999999
XBLNR Number Interval
0000000000000000
to
ZZZZZZZZZZZZZZZZ
Bundling
Items per Bundle
Output Control
☐ Execute as background job
☑ Print Bank Statement
☑ Print Posting Log
☑ Print Statistics

Figure 5.43: Input screen to post internal bank statements to SAP general ledger

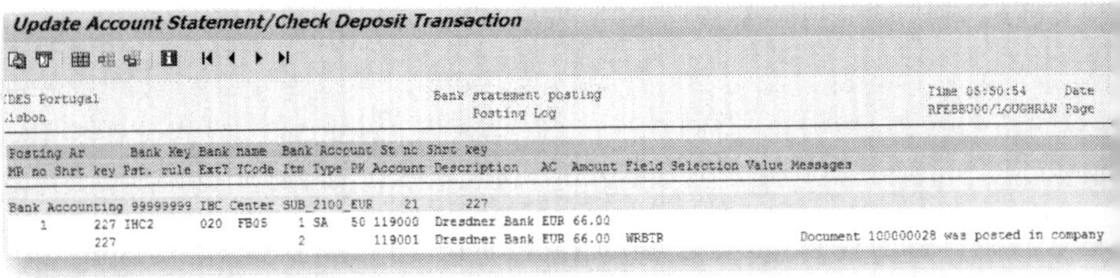
Update Account Statement/Check Deposit Transaction
DES Portugal
isbon
Bank statement posting
Posting Log
Time 05:50:54 Date
RFEBBU00/LOUGHRAN Page
Posting Ar Bank Key Bank name Bank Account St no Shrt key
MR no Shrt key Pst. rule ExtT TCode Itm Type PK Account Description AC Amount Field Selection Value Messages
Bank Accounting 99999999 IHC Center SUB_2100_EUR 21 227
1 227 IHC2 020 FB05 1 SA 50 119000 Dresdner Bank EUR 66.00
227 2 119001 Dresdner Bank EUR 66.00 WRBTR Document 100000028 was posted in company

Figure 5.44: Internal bank statement posting

The other relevant aspect of the end-of-day process is the posting of the IHC current accounts to the SAP general ledger under company code 3010 (i.e. the company code under which the in-house bank resides).

In the second part of the end-of-day process, the IHC activity is posted to the SAP general ledger. Posting the accounting entries for the IHC activity is a two-step process. The first step is the balance sheet preparation (see Figure 5.45), which consolidates the total change in balance, negative or positive, for each account for the day or since the last end-of-day processing steps were run. No actual posting is made during the balance sheet preparation run. The posting is prepared in this step but is not made to the SAP general ledger until the FI transfer step. The second step is to run the FI transfer, which consolidates all activities in each IHC account into groups based on several characteristics.

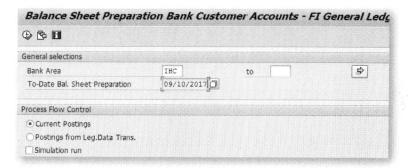

Figure 5.45: IHC balance sheet preparation program input screen

Figure 5.46 shows the output screen for the balance sheet preparation step.

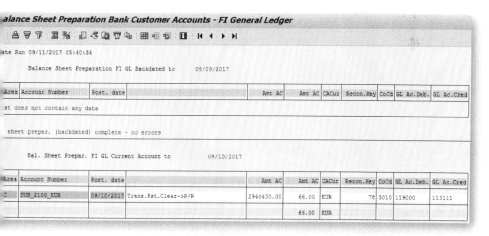

Figure 5.46: Balance sheet preparation program output screen

Figure 5.47 shows the FI transfer input screen.

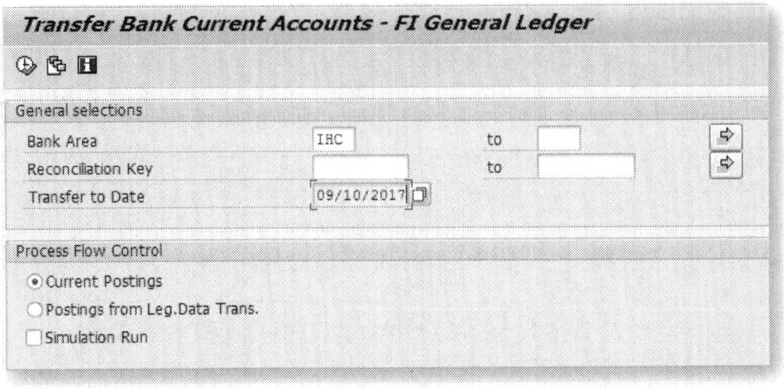

Figure 5.47: FI transfer program input screen

Figure 5.48 shows the FI transfer output screen.

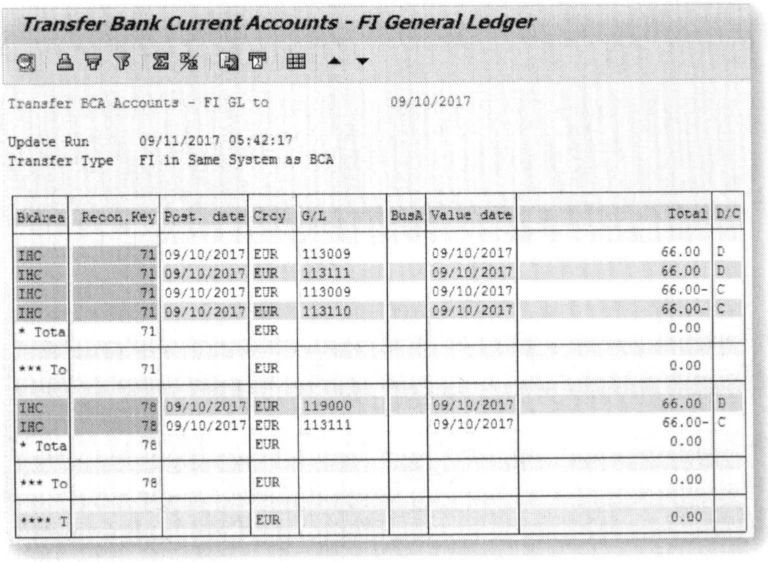

Figure 5.48: FI transfer program output screen

The following shows the net result of the end-of-day postings for the 66 EUR payment on behalf of:

Dr 3010/119000 IHC I/C Balance (trading partn. 2100) 66 EUR

Cr 3010/113110 IHC External Payment Clearing 66 EUR

The debit to the 3010/119000 account records the amount subsidiary 2100 owes the IHB. The credit to the 3010/113110 account offsets the debit made to that account when the external payment was executed by the IHB. (See Step 5 – when the debit was made to the 3010/113110 account.)

Step 9: On the next business day, the in-house bank's external bank statement for the EUR bank account is processed in SAP in the in-house bank's company code, and it records the 66 EUR payment as cleared.

Figure 5.49 shows a sample bank statement for the 66 EUR payment from the IHB.

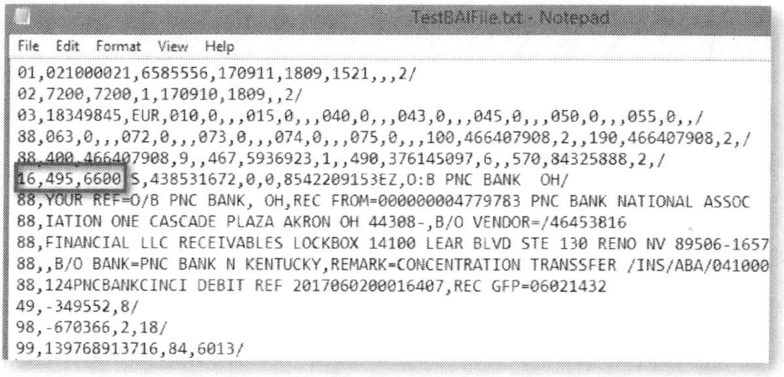
TestBAIFile.txt - Notepad

File Edit Format View Help

```
01,021000021,6585556,170911,1809,1521,,,2/
02,7200,7200,1,170910,1809,,2/
03,18349845,EUR,010,0,,,015,0,,,040,0,,,043,0,,,045,0,,,050,0,,,055,0,,/
88,063,0,,,072,0,,,073,0,,,074,0,,,075,0,,,100,466407908,2,,190,466407908,2,/
88,400,466407908,9,,467,5936923,1,,490,376145097,6,,570,84325888,2,/
16,495,6600 S,438531672,0,0,8542209153EZ,O:B PNC BANK  OH/
88,YOUR REF=O/B PNC BANK, OH,REC FROM=000000004779783 PNC BANK NATIONAL ASSOC
88,IATION ONE CASCADE PLAZA AKRON OH 44308-,B/O VENDOR=/46453816
88,FINANCIAL LLC RECEIVABLES LOCKBOX 14100 LEAR BLVD STE 130 RENO NV 89506-1657
88,,B/O BANK=PNC BANK N KENTUCKY,REMARK=CONCENTRATION TRANSSFER /INS/ABA/041000
88,124PNCBANKCINCI DEBIT REF 201706020016407,REC GFP=06021432
49,-349552,8/
98,-670366,2,18/
99,139768913716,84,6013/
```

Figure 5.49: Sample BAI formatted file for payment on behalf of

The sample bank statement, shown in Figure 5.49, is imported into SAP by following the menu path: ACCOUNTING • FINANCIAL ACCOUNTING • BANKS • INPUT • BANK STATEMENT • IMPORT, or by executing transaction code FF_5 (see Figure 5.50).

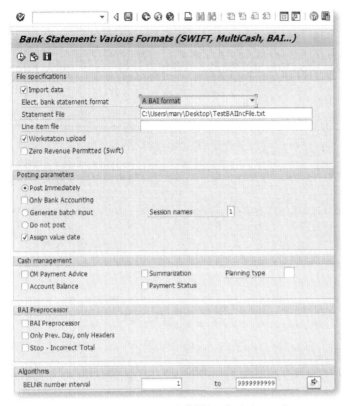

Figure 5.50: Import external bank BAI bank statement

After the import bank statement program is executed, the user sees a screen similar to the one shown in Figure 5.51, recording to the SAP general ledger that the 66 EUR payment has cleared the bank.

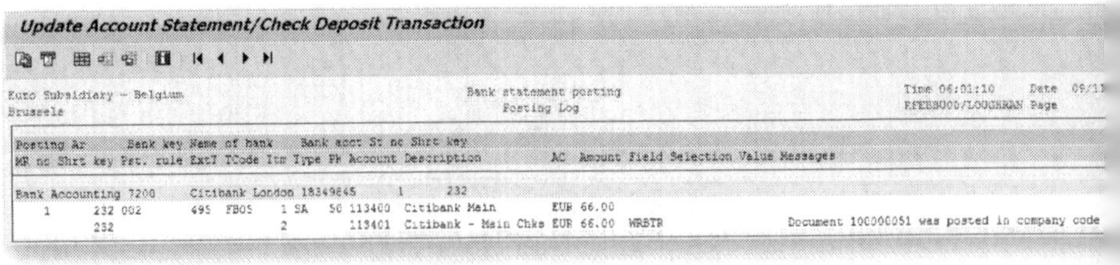

Figure 5.51: External bank statement imported successfully

5.3 Intercompany payments

In our intercompany payments example, subsidiary 2300 delivers services to subsidiary 2100. In the example, the AR and AP invoices are entered into SAP, then subsidiary 2100 triggers the payment through the in-house bank on the netting day. There are no external payments made in this example. The intercompany settlement process for these two entities is executed without the use of an external bank. Although our example involves just two company codes, the same process could be carried out for all company codes in countries where there are no restrictions to net settlement and/or the use of an in-house bank.

Before covering the process flow, let's review the customer and vendor master record settings required for intercompany payments sent through an in-house bank.

In the intercompany vendor master record, the bank details are the IHB bank key and current account for subsidiary 2300. Note that in Figure 5.52 the CTRY, BANK KEY and BANK ACCOUNT fields are populated with the in-house bank's current account for subsidiary 2300.

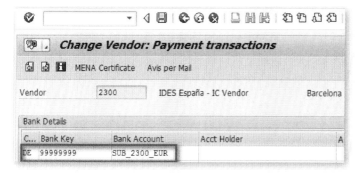

Figure 5.52: Intercompany vendor 2300's bank details

The bank account details entered into the intercompany vendor master record are the same bank details specified for the in-house bank house bank account under company code 2300, as shown in Figure 5.53.

Figure 5.53: Company code 2300's IHC account

In the intercompany vendor master record, payment method I is specified; i.e. the IHC intercompany payment method. IHC is specified as the house bank to be used for payments from 2100 to the intercompany vendor 2300, as shown in Figure 5.54.

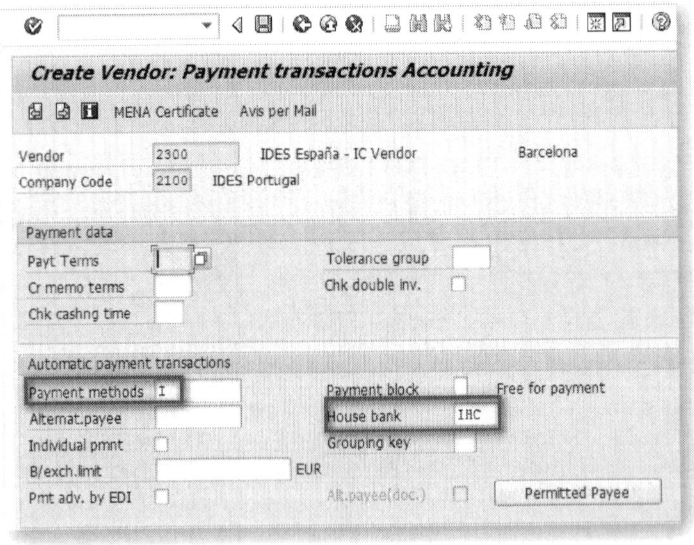

Figure 5.54: Payment information in IC vendor master record

For convenience, the intercompany payments process flow diagram from Figure 3.6 is repeated in Figure 5.55.

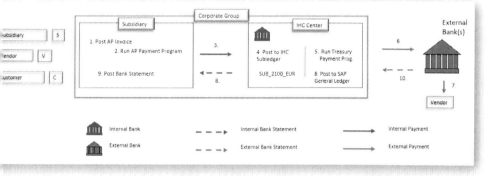

Figure 5.55: Intercompany payments process flow

Before moving on to the example, let's check the balances in the IHC current accounts for subsidiaries 2300 and 2100. We do this by following the menu path: ACCOUNTING • FINANCIAL SUPPLY CHAIN MANAGEMENT • IN-HOUSE CASH • INFORMATION SYSTEM • BALANCE LIST BY KEY DATE or by executing transaction code F970_VAL. This report displays the current balance amount in the IHC current accounts, as shown in Figure 5.56.

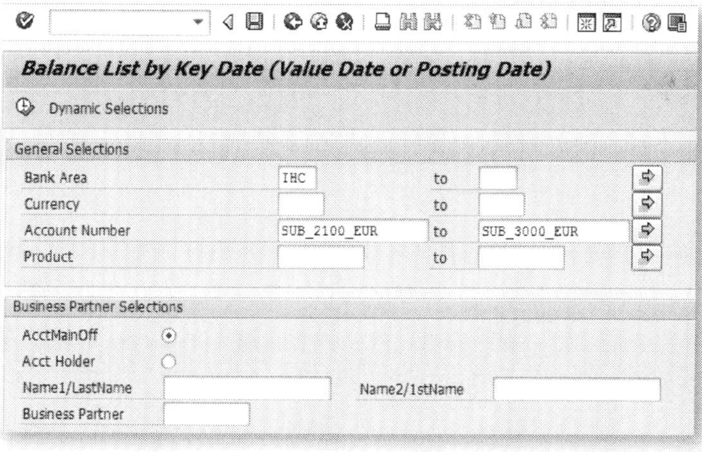

Figure 5.56: Input screen to view IHC current account balances

Figure 5.57 shows the output of the Balance List by Key Date report. We can see that the balance in the current accounts for subsidiaries 2300 and 2100 is zero.

Balance List by Key Date (Value Date or Posting Date)

09/03/2017 02:18:04   Bal. List by   09/03/2017

BkArea	Account Number	Acct Holder	Currency	Balance	Val.Dt.Bal.
IHC	SUB_2300_EUR	IDES Espana, Madrid	EUR	0.00	0.00
IHC	SUB_2900_USD	IDES Espana, Madrid	EUR	0.00	0.00
IHC	SUB_2500_EUR	IDES Netherlands, Rotterdam	EUR	33,745.00-	33,745.00-
IHC	SUB_2100_EUR	IDES Portugal, Lisbon	EUR	0.00	0.00
* IHC			EUR	33,745.00-	
**			EUR	33,745.00-	
IHC	SUB_2900_SEK	IDES Sweden, stockholm	SEK	0.00	0.00
* IHC			SEK	0.00	
**			SEK	0.00	
IHC	SUB_2900_USD	IDES US INC, Chicago	USD	0.00	0.00
* IHC			USD	0.00	
**			USD	0.00	
***			EUR	33,745.00-	
			SEK	0.00	
			USD	0.00	

Figure 5.57: Review IHC current account balances

We'll now walk through the steps in the intercompany payments process in SAP that were outlined in Section 3.2.

Step 1: After subsidiary 2300 delivers services to subsidiary 2100, subsidiary 2300 enters the IC AR invoice into SAP, and sends it to subsidiary 2100 to request payment. The AR invoice is entered into SAP by following the menu path: ACCOUNTING • FINANCIAL ACCOUNTING • ACCOUNTS RECEIVABLE • DOCUMENT ENTRY • INVOICE, or by executing transaction code FB70 (see Figure 5.58).

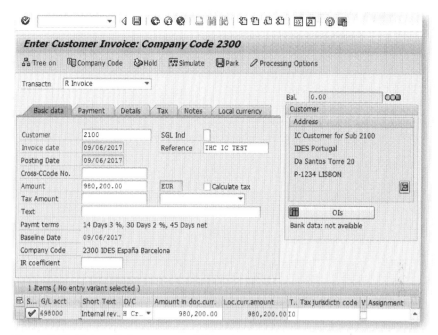

Figure 5.58: Entry of intercompany AR invoice

When the invoice is saved, the following message is displayed:

☑ Document 1800000007 was posted in company code 2300 .

Step 2: Next, subsidiary 2100 enters the AP invoice into SAP. The AP invoice is entered into SAP by following the menu path: ACCOUNTING • FINANCIAL ACCOUNTING • ACCOUNTS PAYABLE • DOCUMENT ENTRY • IN-VOICE, or by executing transaction code FB60 (see Figure 5.59). Note how the I/C customer invoice is entered in the invoice number (REFER-ENCE) field. This enables automatic clearing for the IHC bank statement subledger postings.

Note that in the PAYMENT tab of the invoice entry screen in Figure 5.60, the payment method in the AP invoice is payment method I, which has a payment medium format of a payment IDoc. This payment IDoc is sent from subsidiary 2100 to the in-house bank, when the AP payment program is executed for subsidiary 2100.

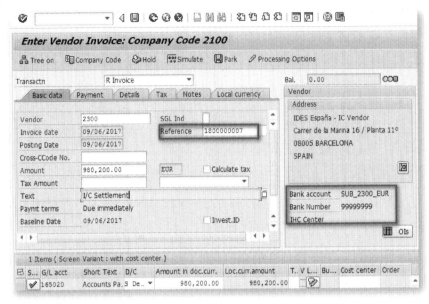

Figure 5.59: Enter intercompany AP invoice in 2100

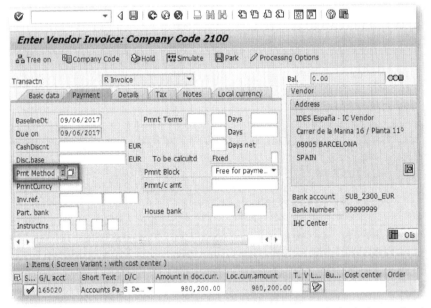

Figure 5.60: AP invoice has payment method I to route through the in-house bank

Step 3: On the agreed netting day, subsidiary 2100 initiates an internal settlement by running the AP payment program, which can be found by following the menu path: ACCOUNTING • FINANCIAL ACCOUNTING • ACCOUNTS PAYABLE • PERIODIC PROCESSING • PAYMENTS, or by executing transaction code F110. This sends payment details to the in-house bank for processing and, at the same time, the intercompany payable is cleared under company code 2100. Since the steps to run the AP payment program were outlined in detail in the "Payment on behalf of" section of this chapter, the detailed steps are not provided here. Figure 5.61 shows the payment parameters of the AP payment program run.

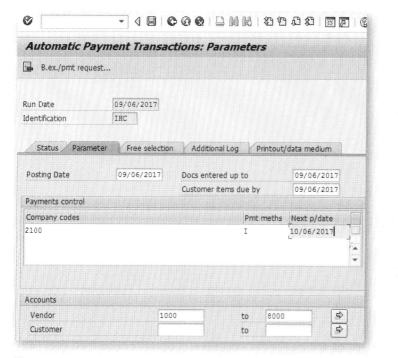

Figure 5.61: Payment parameters for AP payment program for intercompany payment

Figure 5.62 shows the successfully completed AP payment run.

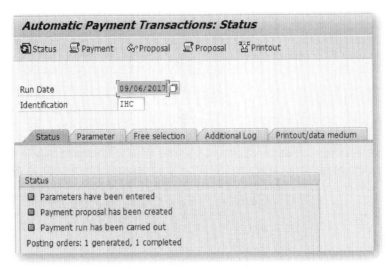

Figure 5.62: Successful run of the AP payment program for intercompany payment

The payment details are sent from subsidiary 2100 to the in-house bank in the form of a PAYEXT IDoc. Figure 5.63 shows the PAYEXT IDocs generated for this intercompany payment. The contents of the two IDocs are the same. The outbound IDoc is sent from subsidiary 2100 and the inbound IDoc is sent to the in-house bank. A reason for the two IDocs is that the IHC module can work across multiple SAP instances. In our example scenarios, however, the IHB and the participating subsidiaries are in the same SAP instance.

Figure 5.63: Payment IDoc sent from subsidiary to IHB

Drilling down into the inbound IDoc, we can see that the sending bank account in the E1IDB02 BA segment is the IHC current account in subsidiary 2100, as shown in Figure 5.64. This is the IHC current account that is debited when posting the IHC payment order.

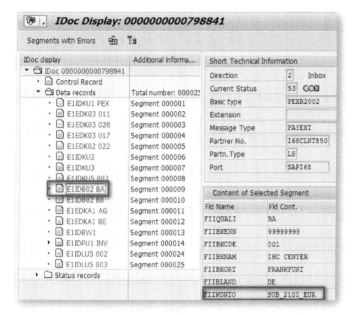

Figure 5.64: Source bank account in inbound payment IDoc

In Figure 5.65, we see the recipient bank account information in the E1IDB02 BB segment, which shows that the target or beneficiary's bank account information is subsidiary 2300's in-house cash current account. This is the IHC current account that is credited when posting the IHC payment order.

The accounting entries made under company code 2100 when the AP payment program is run are a debit to the intercompany vendor representing subsidiary 2300, and a credit to the IHC cash clearing account. These can be seen by reviewing the payment run log, which is viewed by pressing the 🗐 Payment button from F110 (see Figure 5.66).

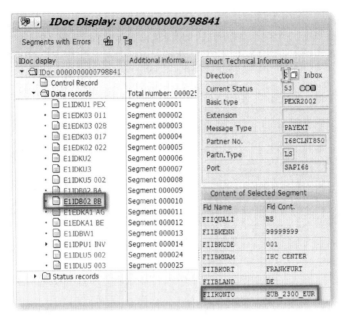

Figure 5.65: Target bank account in inbound payment IDoc

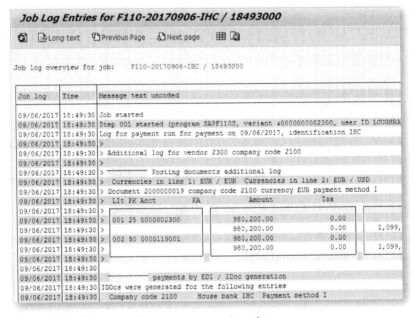

Figure 5.66: AP payment program payment run log

Step 4: When the in-house bank processes the PAYEXT payment IDoc from subsidiary 2100, it automatically determines that the payment is an internal/intercompany payment and creates a payment order that debits the current account of subsidiary 2100 and credits the current account of subsidiary 2300 in the amount of the payment.

When the payment order is initially created, it is created in the status of FLAGGED FOR POSTING. This status is comparable to a parked FI document. The payment order can be viewed by following the menu path: ACCOUNTING • FINANCIAL SUPPLY CHAIN MANAGEMENT • IN-HOUSE CASH • ACCOUNT MANAGEMENT • IHC PAYMENT ORDERS • PAYMENT ORDER BROWSER, or by executing transaction code IHC0 (see Figure 5.67). Note that because this is an internal payment order, the payment order transaction type is IPF.

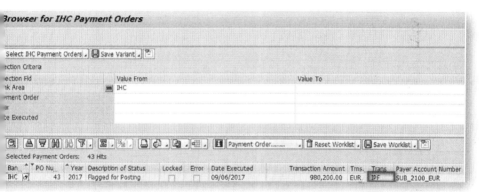

Figure 5.67: Internal payment order flagged for posting

By selecting the payment order, right clicking and selecting POST from the menu, the payment order is posted to the subledger, as shown in Figure 5.68. At this point, the IHC current accounts are updated with this payment; however, the IHC activity is not posted to the SAP general ledger until the end-of-day process is run.

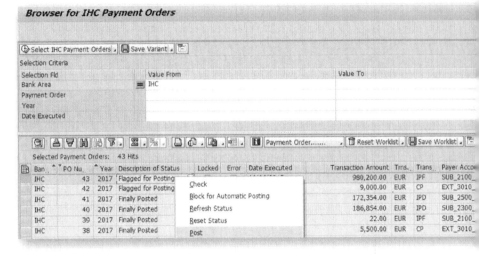

Figure 5.68: Post internal payment order to IHC subledger

After pressing the POST option from the popup-menu, the user receives the popup message shown in Figure 5.69.

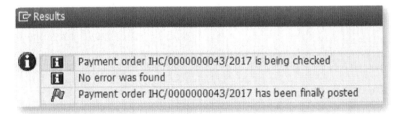

Figure 5.69: Informational message that payment order is finally posted

By double-clicking on the payment order from transaction code IHC0, the OVERVIEW tab of the payment order is displayed, as shown in Figure 5.70.

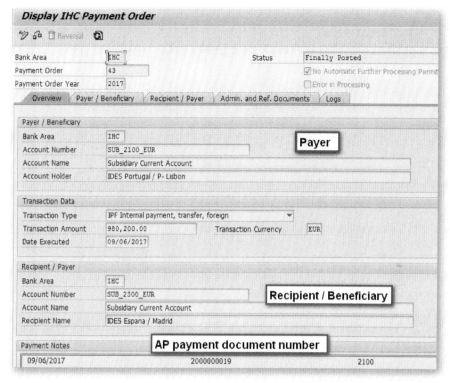

Figure 5.70: Drilldown on payment order from IHC0

Step 5: The in-house bank's end-of-day process is run, during which an internal bank statement is sent from the in-house bank to each of the subsidiaries containing activity processed at the IHB for the day. The bank statement is sent to the subsidiaries electronically in the form of a FINSTA IDoc. A second activity that occurs when running the IHC end-of-day process is the posting of the day's IHC activity to the SAP general ledger of the company code where the IHB resides, which is company code 3010. The IHB records a payable for subsidiary 2100 and a receivable for subsidiary 2300.

The full end-of-day processing steps are shown in more detail in Section 5.6 of this chapter, but the two steps mentioned above have been covered in order to show the end-to-end process.

The input of the balance sheet preparation step is shown in Figure 5.71.

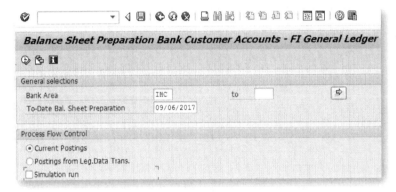

Figure 5.71: Balance sheet preparation program input screen

The output of the balance sheet preparation step is shown in Figure 5.72.

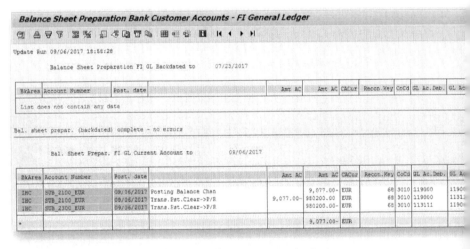

Figure 5.72: Balance sheet preparation program output screen

The input of the FI transfer step is shown in Figure 5.73.

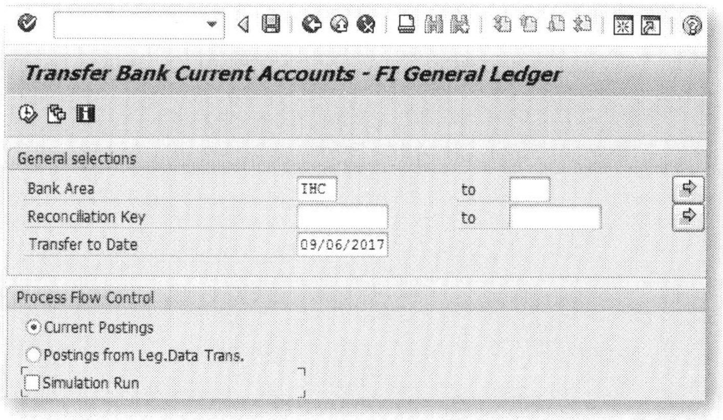

Figure 5.73: Input screen to FI transfer program

The output of the FI transfer step is shown in Figure 5.74.

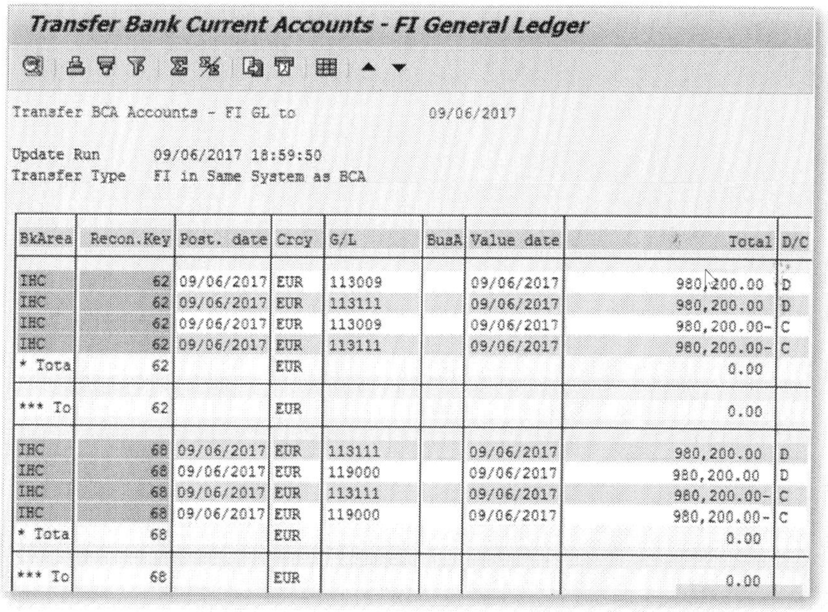
Transfer Bank Current Accounts - FI General Ledger

Transfer BCA Accounts - FI GL to 09/06/2017

Update Run 09/06/2017 18:59:50
Transfer Type FI in Same System as BCA

BkArea	Recon.Key	Post. date	Crcy	G/L	BusA	Value date	Total	D/C
IHC	62	09/06/2017	EUR	113009		09/06/2017	980,200.00	D
IHC	62	09/06/2017	EUR	113111		09/06/2017	980,200.00	D
IHC	62	09/06/2017	EUR	113009		09/06/2017	980,200.00-	C
IHC	62	09/06/2017	EUR	113111		09/06/2017	980,200.00-	C
* Tota	62		EUR				0.00	
*** To	62		EUR				0.00	
IHC	68	09/06/2017	EUR	113111		09/06/2017	980,200.00	D
IHC	68	09/06/2017	EUR	119000		09/06/2017	980,200.00	D
IHC	68	09/06/2017	EUR	113111		09/06/2017	980,200.00-	C
IHC	68	09/06/2017	EUR	119000		09/06/2017	980,200.00-	C
* Tota	68		EUR				0.00	
*** To	68		EUR				0.00	

Figure 5.74: Output screen to FI transfer program

The IHC accounting entries can be difficult to follow due to the postings to the various clearing accounts. The net postings made to the SAP general ledger under company code 3010 for the intercompany payment are summarized as follows:

Dr 3010/119000 IHC I/C Balance (trading partner 2100)

  Cr 3010/119000 IHC I/C Balance (trading partner 2300)

SAP's IHC module was built for a high-volume of transactions, which is why it posts to the SAP general ledger through reconciliation keys.

Step 6: When the IHC end-of-day process is run, bank statements are sent to each of the subsidiaries. The bank statements hold the activity for the corresponding current accounts for the previous day, in the same way as if the payments had been executed at an external bank. The accounting entries made under company code 2300 are a debit to the IHC cash clearing account, and a credit the IHC balance G/L account. The accounting entries made under company code 2100 are a debit to the IHC bank balance G/L account, and a credit to the IHC cash clearing account. In addition, the IC AR invoice is cleared under company code 2300. Figure 5.75 shows the posting of the internal bank statements to the SAP general ledger.

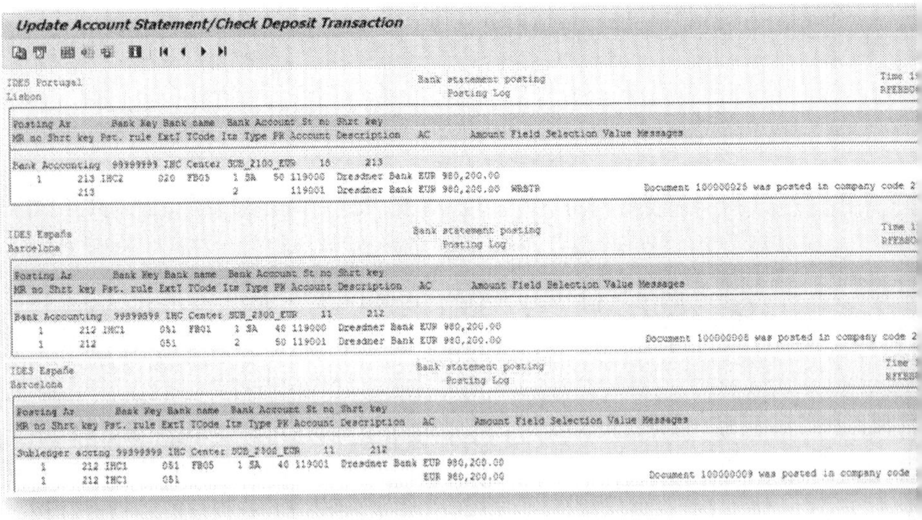

Figure 5.75: Internal bank statement postings

After executing the intercompany payment scenario, we check the balances in the IHC current accounts for subsidiaries 2300 and 2100. We do this by following the menu path: ACCOUNTING • FINANCIAL SUPPLY CHAIN MANAGEMENT • IN-HOUSE CASH • INFORMATION SYSTEM • BALANCE LIST BY KEY DATE or by executing transaction code F970_VAL. This report shows the current balance amount in the IHC current accounts (see Figure 5.76).

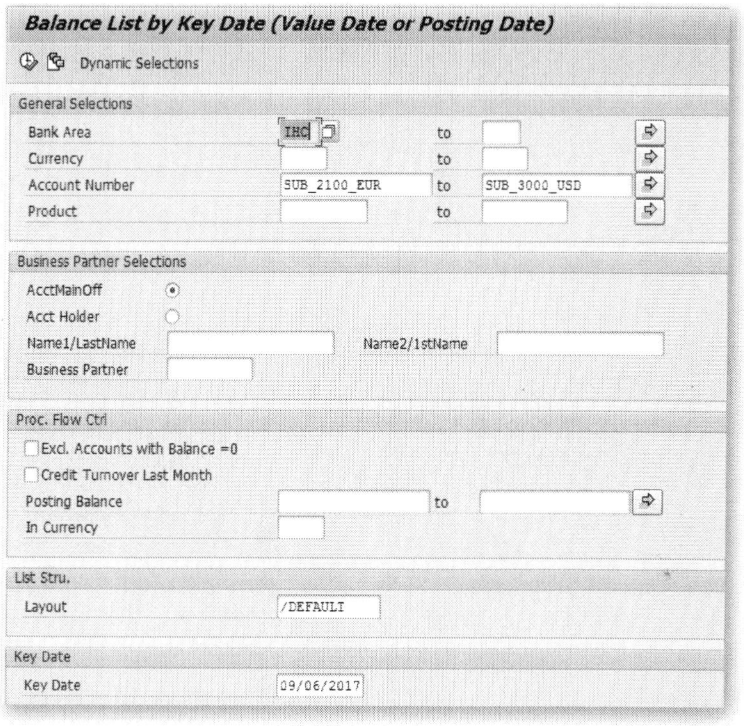

Figure 5.76: Input screen to the Balance List by Key Date report

Figure 5.77 shows the output screen of the Balance List by Key Date report. We can see that the balance in the current accounts for subsidiaries 2300 and 2100 reflect the completed intercompany payment.

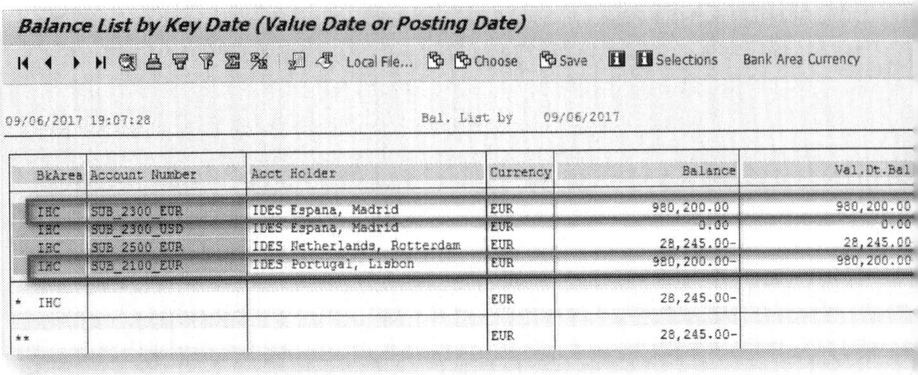

Figure 5.77: Balance List by Key Date report output screen

5.4 Collections on behalf of

Collections on behalf of (also known as centralized receipts, receivables on behalf of, or ROBO payments) take place when external business partners or customers make payments to a centralized bank account, which in our case is an IHB bank account, in order to clear receivables in a subsidiary of the receiving company.

This process is initiated when an external party, typically a customer, makes a payment to a bank account owned by the in-house bank. The in-house bank receives the payment, creates a payment order that credits the subsidiary's current account, then passes it along to the appropriate subsidiary in the internal bank statement.

Before getting started, check the balance in subsidiary 2100's IHC current account by using the Balance List by Key Date report (transaction code F970_VAL). The balance is negative **2,949,573.00 EUR**, as shown in Figure 5.78.

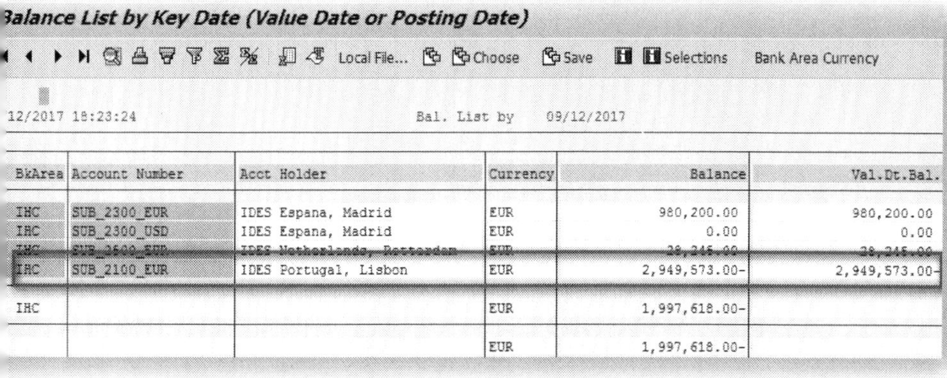

Balance List by Key Date (Value Date or Posting Date)

◀ ◀ ▶ ▶ ⬚ 🖨 ▽ ▽ Σ ⅌ ⬚ ⬚ Local File... 🗐 🗐 Choose 🗐 Save 🔢 🔢 Selections   Bank Area Currency

12/2017 18:23:24   Bal. List by   09/12/2017

BkArea	Account Number	Acct Holder	Currency	Balance	Val.Dt.Bal.
IHC	SUB_2300_EUR	IDES Espana, Madrid	EUR	980,200.00	980,200.00
IHC	SUB_2300_USD	IDES Espana, Madrid	EUR	0.00	0.00
IHC	SUB_2600_EUR	IDES Netherlands, Rotterdam	EUR	28,245.00	28,245.00
IHC	SUB_2100_EUR	IDES Portugal, Lisbon	EUR	2,949,573.00-	2,949,573.00-
IHC			EUR	1,997,618.00-	
			EUR	1,997,618.00-	

Figure 5.78: Balance List by Key Date report output screen

We will now walk through the six steps in this process:

Step 1: An external customer sends a payment to an external bank account associated with the IHB. This takes place at the external bank.

Step 2: The payment is received in the bank statement from the IHB's external bank, which in our case is a BAI formatted bank statement with an incoming wire (see Figure 5.79). The "note to payee" information for this payment contains the key text COMP2100 to trigger a centralized payment on behalf of payment order.

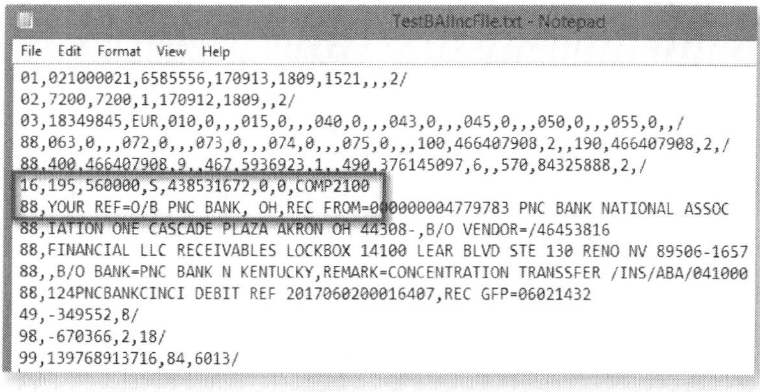

```
TestBAIncFile.txt - Notepad
File  Edit  Format  View  Help
01,021000021,6585556,170913,1809,1521,,,2/
02,7200,7200,1,170912,1809,,2/
03,18349845,EUR,010,0,,,015,0,,,040,0,,,043,0,,,045,0,,,050,0,,,055,0,,/
88,063,0,,,072,0,,,073,0,,,074,0,,,075,0,,,100,466407908,2,,190,466407908,2,/
88,400,466407908,9,,467,5936923,1,,490,376145097,6,,570,84325888,2,/
16,195,560000,S,438531672,0,0,COMP2100
88,YOUR REF=O/B PNC BANK, OH,REC FROM=000000004779783 PNC BANK NATIONAL ASSOC
88,IATION ONE CASCADE PLAZA AKRON OH 44308-,B/O VENDOR=/46453816
88,FINANCIAL LLC RECEIVABLES LOCKBOX 14100 LEAR BLVD STE 130 RENO NV 89506-1657
88,,B/O BANK=PNC BANK N KENTUCKY,REMARK=CONCENTRATION TRANSSFER /INS/ABA/041000
88,124PNCBANKCINCI DEBIT REF 2017060200016407,REC GFP=06021432
49,-349552,8/
98,-670366,2,18/
99,139768913716,84,6013/
```

Figure 5.79: BAI file containing key text to trigger payment order

Step 3: When the external bank statement is posted to the SAP general ledger, SAP debits the main G/L account for the external house bank account, and credits the IHC external clearing account by an electronic bank statement search string.

The SAP program to import bank statements can be found by following the menu path: ACCOUNTING • FINANCIAL ACCOUNTING • BANKS • INPUT • BANK STATEMENT • IMPORT, or by executing transaction code FF_5 (see Figure 5.80).

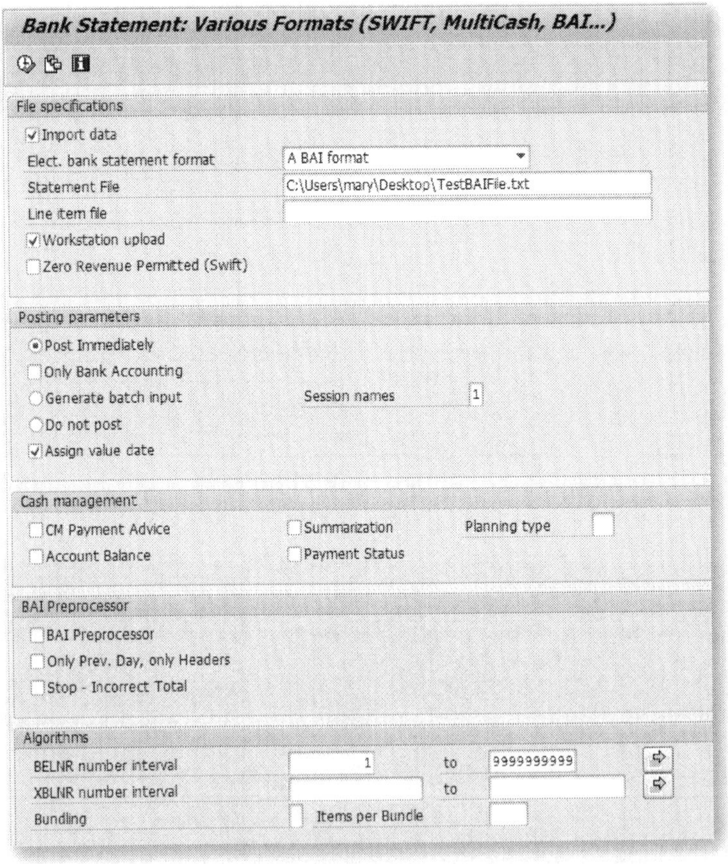

Figure 5.80: Import BAI file containing centralized payment order

After pressing the execute icon ⊕, the bank statement is imported into SAP; Figure 5.81 shows the screen which is then displayed. Note the message that payment order 61 has been created.

Figure 5.81: Postings from importing external bank statement

Step 4: The IHB recognizes the incoming payment as belonging to subsidiary 2100, and so creates a payment order that credits the IHB current account for subsidiary 2100 and debits the IHB's external payments clearing account. The payment order status is initially FLAGGED FOR POSTING. To post the payment order to the IHC subledger, select the payment order, right-click on it, and select POST from the menu, as shown in Figure 5.82.

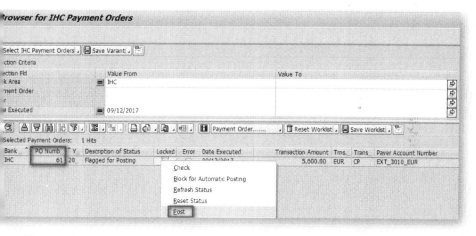

Figure 5.82: Post centralized incoming payment using IHC0

By drilling down on the centralized incoming payment order, we can see the relevant details of it, as shown in Figure 5.83. Note that the full note to payee text from the bank statement is carried forward to the PAYMENT NOTES field in the payment order.

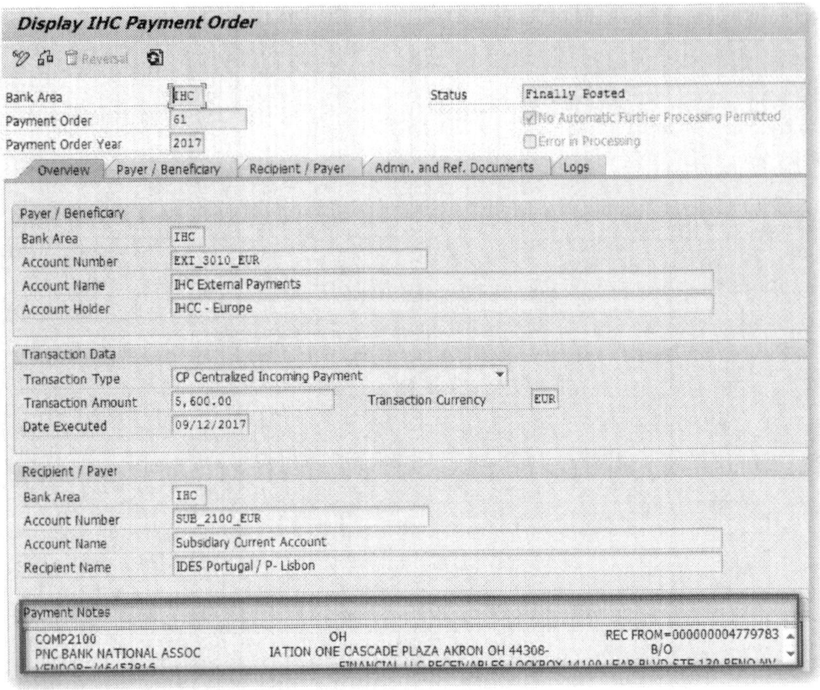

Figure 5.83: Centralized incoming payment order

Step 5: As part of the end-of-day process chain, the IHC activity is post-ed to the SAP general ledger, and internal bank statements are sent. Although the two processes are independent, we post to the SAP gen-eral ledger first. Keep in mind that the end-of-day process should be scheduled daily.

When the IHC end-of-day process is run, the IHC activity for the day is posted to the SAP general ledger of the company code where the IHB resides, which is company code 3010 in our example.

Posting the accounting entries for the IHC activity is a two-step process. The first step is the balance sheet preparation, followed by the FI trans-fer step. As these two steps are detailed in Sections 3.5 and 5.6, for the ROBO payment, the screenshots are displayed here without detailed explanations.

Figure 5.84 shows the input screen for the balance sheet preparation program.

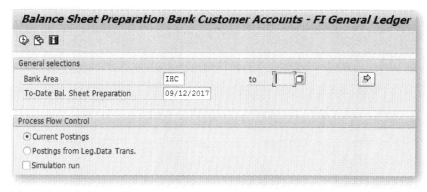

Figure 5.84: Balance sheet preparation input screen

Figure 5.85 shows the posting entries that are made as part of the balance sheet preparation step. In this step, the postings are prepared, but do not post to the SAP general ledger until the FI transfer program is run.

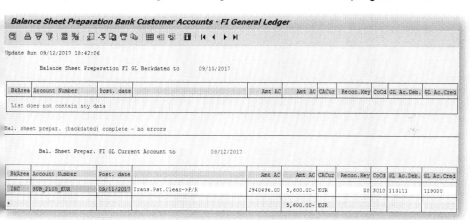

Figure 5.85: Balance sheet preparation output screen

Figure 5.86 shows the input screen to the FI transfer program.

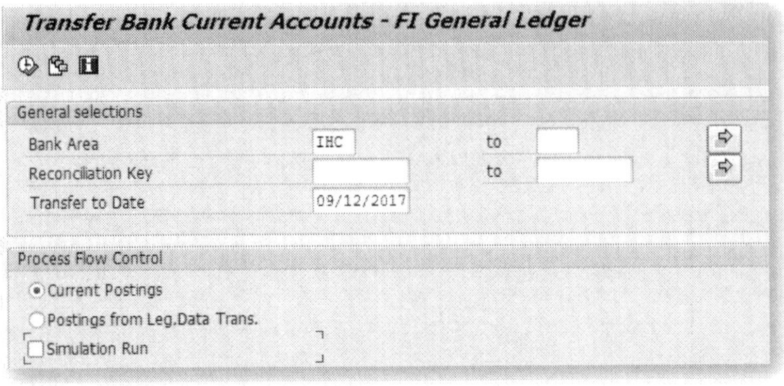

Transfer Bank Current Accounts - FI General Ledger

General selections

Bank Area	IHC	to	
Reconciliation Key		to	
Transfer to Date	09/12/2017		

Process Flow Control

- ● Current Postings
- ○ Postings from Leg.Data Trans.
- ☐ Simulation Run

Figure 5.86: Input screen to the FI transfer program

Figure 5.87 shows the posting entries that are made as part of the FI transfer step.

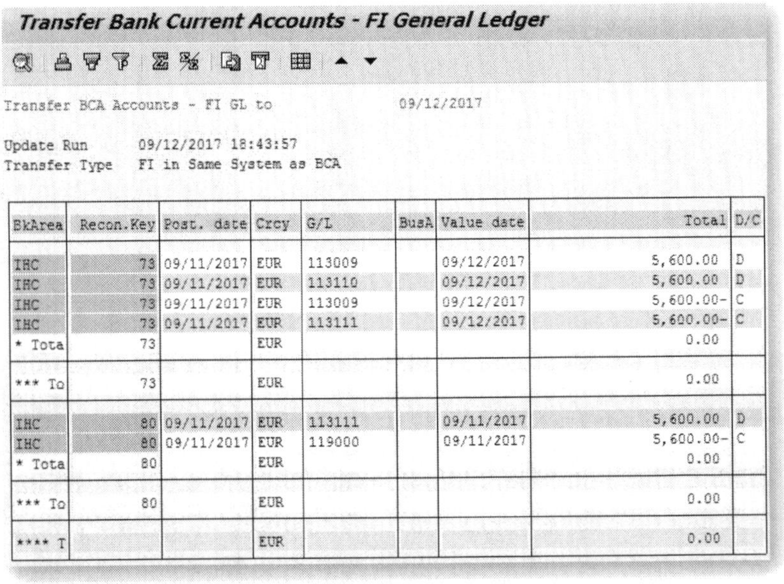

Transfer Bank Current Accounts - FI General Ledger

Transfer BCA Accounts - FI GL to   09/12/2017

Update Run   09/12/2017 18:43:57
Transfer Type   FI in Same System as BCA

BkArea	Recon.Key	Post. date	Crcy	G/L	BusA	Value date	Total	D/C
IHC	73	09/11/2017	EUR	113009		09/12/2017	5,600.00	D
IHC	73	09/11/2017	EUR	113110		09/12/2017	5,600.00	D
IHC	73	09/11/2017	EUR	113009		09/12/2017	5,600.00-	C
IHC	73	09/11/2017	EUR	113111		09/12/2017	5,600.00-	C
* Tota	73		EUR				0.00	
*** To	73		EUR				0.00	
IHC	80	09/11/2017	EUR	113111		09/11/2017	5,600.00	D
IHC	80	09/11/2017	EUR	119000		09/11/2017	5,600.00-	C
* Tota	80		EUR				0.00	
*** To	80		EUR				0.00	
**** T			EUR				0.00	

Figure 5.87: Output screen to the FI transfer program

The net postings as part of the end-of-day process are the following:

Dr 3010/113110 IHC External Payment Clearing

   Cr 3010/119000 IHC I/C Balance (trading partner 2100)

Next, an internal bank statement is sent from the in-house bank to each of the subsidiaries containing activities processed at the IHB that day. Note: the internal bank statements can be sent before or after the IHC activity is posted to the SAP general ledger.

The internal bank statements are sent by following the menu path: AC-COUNTING • FINANCIAL SUPPLY CHAIN MANAGEMENT • IN-HOUSE CASH • PERIODIC PROCESSING • BANK STATEMENT • NEW RUN • MASS RUN, or by executing transaction code F9N1 (see Figure 5.88).

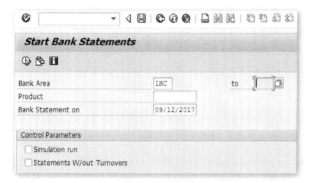

Figure 5.88: Mass sending of the IHC internal bank statements

After F9N1 is executed, the message in Figure 5.89 is displayed.

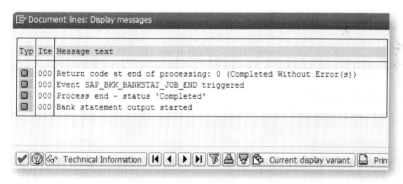

Figure 5.89: Informational message on bank statements

Step 6: As the bank statement is posted in the subsidiary, it debits the main G/L account for the in-house bank account and credits a cash clearing account for the internal house bank account. In the bank statement postings process, this step is the area 1 posting (general ledger).

With the area 2 posting (subledger), the cash clearing account for the internal house bank account is debited and a credit is made to the customer account, if the customer can be determined, or to an IHC AR un-applied receipts clearing account.

The internal bank statements are then posted by following the menu path: ACCOUNTING • FINANCIAL ACCOUNTING • BANKS • INPUT • BANK STATEMENT • POST, or by executing transaction code FEBP (see Figure 5.90).

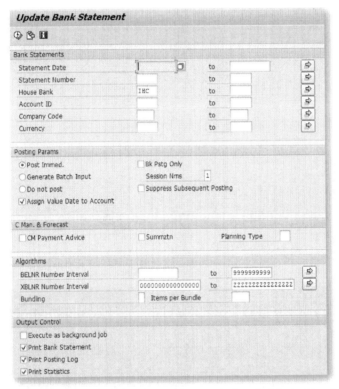

Figure 5.90: Post internal bank statements in subsidiaries' books

Figure 5.91 shows the postings made for the receipt on behalf of trans-action sent to company code 2100. When the receipt posts in 2100, postings for area 1 and 2 are both made. The area 1 posting debits the IHC I/C Balance account (2100/119000) and credits the IHC House Bank Clearing account (2100/119001). The area 2 posting debits the IHC House Bank Clearing account (2100/119001), and credits the customer account or the IHC Unapplied Cash Receipts Clearing account (2100/119005). If posting to the unapplied cash account, a manual post-processing step applies the receipt to the correct customer account.

Figure 5.91: ROBO IHC bank statement subsidiary postings

SAP functionality for post-processing external bank statements is also available for post-processing IHC bank statements. Business users can view the internal bank statements by following the menu path: ACCOUNTING • FINANCIAL ACCOUNTING • BANKS • INPUT • BANK STATEMENT • DISPLAY or by executing transaction code FF.6 (see Figure 5.92).

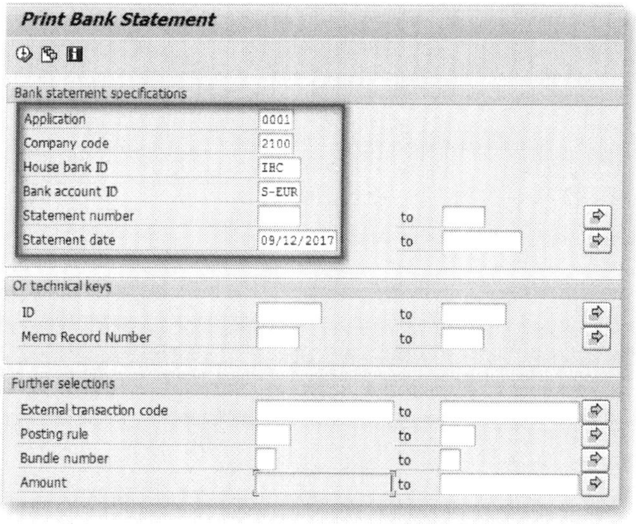

Figure 5.92: View internal bank statement

After entering the inputs for the statement, press the execute icon ⊕ to view the internal bank statement, as shown in Figure 5.93. Note that the full note to payee text received from the external bank is carried forward to the internal bank statement.

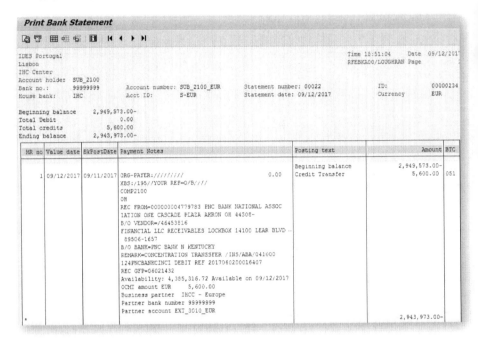

Figure 5.93: View ROBO bank statement transaction

As a final step, check the balance in the SUB_2100_EUR current account after the incoming receipt. The balance in Figure 5.94 has changed by 5,600 EUR, when compared to Figure 5.78.

BkArea	Account Number	Acct Holder	Currency	Balance
IHC	SUB_2300_EUR	IDES Espana, Madrid	EUR	985,200.00
IHC	SUB_2300_USD	IDES Espana, Madrid	EUR	0.00
IHC	SUB_2500_EUR	IDES Netherlands, Rotterdam	EUR	28,245.00-
IHC	SUB_2100_EUR	IDES Portugal, Lisbon	EUR	2,943,973.00-
* IHC			EUR	1,987,018.00-

Figure 5.94: View current balance in SUB_2100_EUR account

5.5   Manual payment orders

As described in Chapter 3, manual payment orders are IHC payments that are initiated at the in-house bank, as opposed to being initiated either by a subsidiary running the AP payment program or an external party sending an incoming payment for a subsidiary to the in-house bank.

Figure 5.96 shows the manual creation of an internal payment order. The payment order posts from one current account to another. There is no external bank account involved in this type of payment order. There are only postings to IHC current accounts.

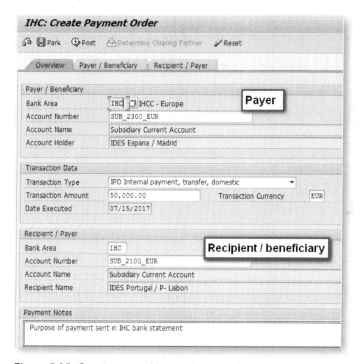

Figure 5.95: Create manual internal payment order

Figure 5.96 shows the manual creation of an external payment order. With this type of payment order, an external payment is made by the in-house bank from an internal current account to an external bank account. In this case, when the payment order is created, a debit is made to the SUB_2300_EUR current account and a payment request is created, generating a payment to the external bank account at ABK Bank.

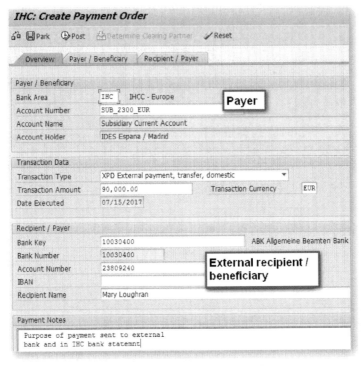

Figure 5.96: Create manual external payment order

After the payment order fields have been updated, the user presses the POST icon ⊕Post, and the payment order IHC current accounts are updated.

In the interest of eliminating repetitive content, we will not look at the end-to-end steps for manual payment orders. The manual payment orders are a shortened version of the corresponding "payment orders generated automatically" processes. The only difference with manual payment orders is that an adjustment accounting entry is needed at the subsidiary, because the AP payment program is not run. The decision would be made at implementation how best to do this; but it could be as easy as making an adjustment entry as part of the EBS post-processing.

5.6   End-of-day processing

All payments processed through the IHC module run through the end-of-day processing steps described here. There are several steps to finalize the IHC activity for a day, such as posting the balances of the IHC current accounts to the SAP general ledger, calculating interest and other fees, as well as creating and generating daily bank statements, which are all tasks a real bank would do.

The IHC end-of-day processing steps can be run manually or can be scheduled; but should be scheduled. Table 3.6 described the steps involved in the IHC end-of-day process in SAP, which we will walk through in detail now.

 Because the end-of-day steps are run frequently (daily), input variants should be created on each of the end-of-day programs. This saves time when running the end-of-day process in testing.

Step 1: The first step in the end-of-day process is to close the current date for IHC processing and move the IHC posting date to the next business day. Any transactions received by the IHB from this point forward receive a posting date of the next business day. This step is performed by following the menu path: ACCOUNTING • FINANCIAL SUPPLY CHAIN MANAGEMENT • IN-HOUSE CASH • PERIODIC PROCESSING • POSTING DATE • PAYMENT TRANSACTIONS or by executing transaction code F9B1, and is shown in Figure 5.97. After the BANK AREA field is populated, SAP populates the two date fields automatically.

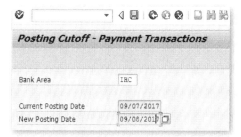

Figure 5.97: Increment the posting cut-off date

After pressing the Save icon 💾, the user sees the popup message displayed in Figure 5.98.

Figure 5.98: Confirmation message on posting date change

After the user presses the YES button, the posting date is moved forward one day and the following message is displayed NEW POSTING DATE 09/08/2017 SET FOR BANK AREA IHC.

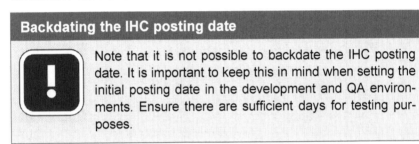

Backdating the IHC posting date

Note that it is not possible to backdate the IHC posting date. It is important to keep this in mind when setting the initial posting date in the development and QA environments. Ensure there are sufficient days for testing purposes.

Step 2: The account balancing transaction codes can be found on the SAP menu under: ACCOUNTING • FINANCIAL SUPPLY CHAIN MANAGEMENT • IN-HOUSE CASH • PERIODIC PROCESSING • ACCOUNT BALANCING • NEW RUN • MASS RUN, or by running transaction code F991 (see Figure 5.99). To run account balancing on one current account only, use the Single Run program or execute transaction code F996.

After the account balancing program is run, the user sees a popup message like the one shown in Figure 5.100.

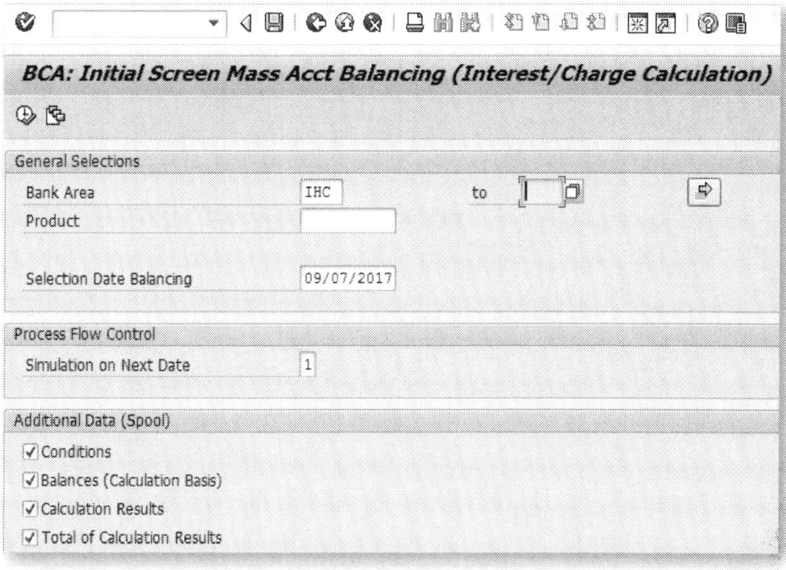

Figure 5.99: IHC mass account balancing program

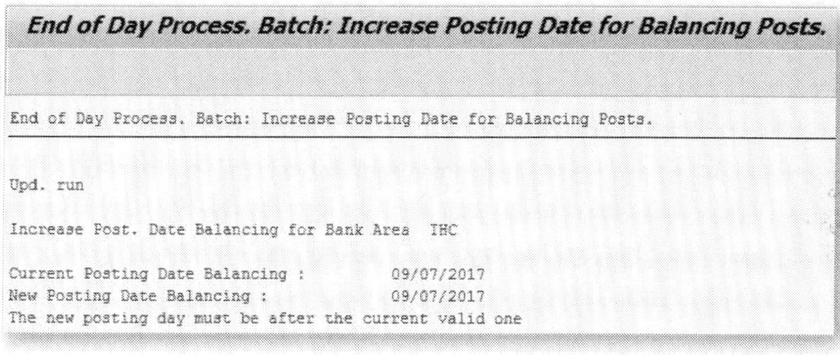

Figure 5.100: Account balancing completion message

How interest is charged on the IHC current accounts is based on how the conditions have been defined in the current accounts on the AC-COUNT BALANCING tab. Figure 5.101 shows the options in the SAP system. However, this is configuration driven, so you have various possibilities: fixed or floating interest, or no interest.

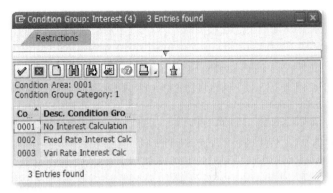

Figure 5.101: Configurable interest conditions

Step 3: After the account balancing program has been executed, the next step is to move the account balancing posting date forward a day. This account balancing posting date should be incremented daily even if an account balancing run has not been executed; e.g. if the accounting balancing takes place as a month-end activity. The POSTING DATE BALANCING field should be set to the next calendar day, as shown in Figure 5.102 and Figure 5.103.

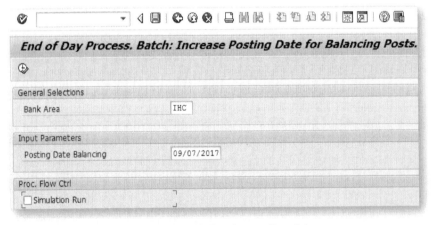

Figure 5.102: Increment the account balancing posting date

Step 4: The next step is to record in the SAP general ledger any payments sent through the IHB since the last end-of-day processing steps were run.

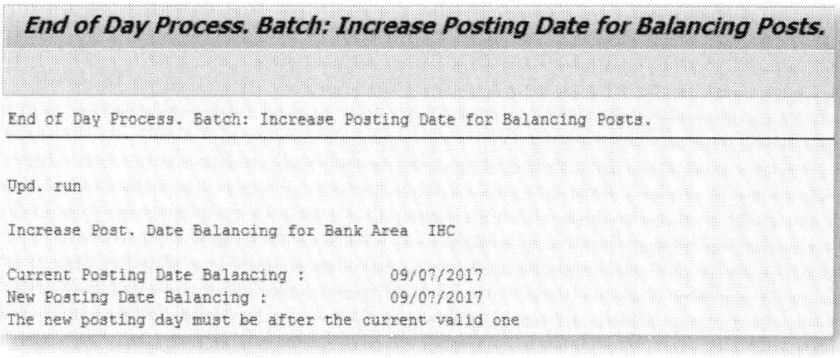

```
End of Day Process. Batch: Increase Posting Date for Balancing Posts.

End of Day Process. Batch: Increase Posting Date for Balancing Posts.

Upd. run

Increase Post. Date Balancing for Bank Area   IHC

Current Posting Date Balancing :          09/07/2017
New Posting Date Balancing :              09/07/2017
The new posting day must be after the current valid one
```

Figure 5.103: Output screen for the account balancing date

Posting the accounting entries for the IHB activity is a two-step process. The first step is the balance sheet preparation, which consolidates the total change in balance, negative or positive, for each account for the day or since the last end-of-day processing steps were run. (If the balance in the IHC account is zero, the balance sheet preparation step does nothing for that current account.) This amount is summarized into a single G/L posting that is made to the SAP general ledger of the bank area. The posting is to the IHC I/C Balance G/L account on one side (account 119000) and the IHC EOD Summary Clearing account (113111) on the other side. This step can be run by following the menu path: ACCOUNTING • FINANCIAL SUPPLY CHAIN MANAGEMENT • IN-HOUSE CASH • PERIODIC PROCESSING • GENERAL LEDGER • BALANCE SHEET PREPARATION, or by executing transaction code F9HI (see Figure 5.104).

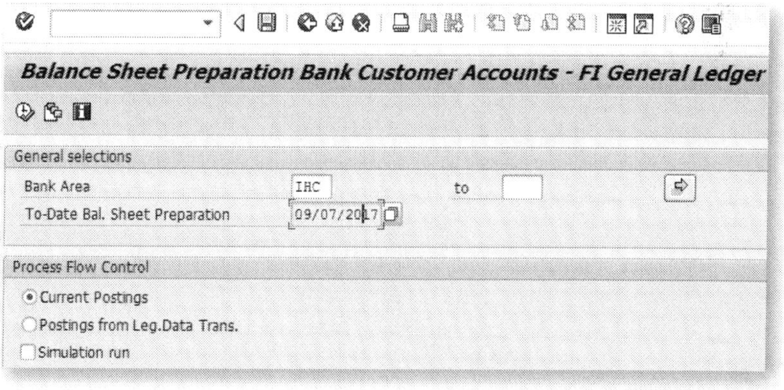

Figure 5.104: Input screen to balance sheet preparation step

After pressing the execute icon ⊕, the postings prepared in this step are displayed, as shown in Figure 5.105.

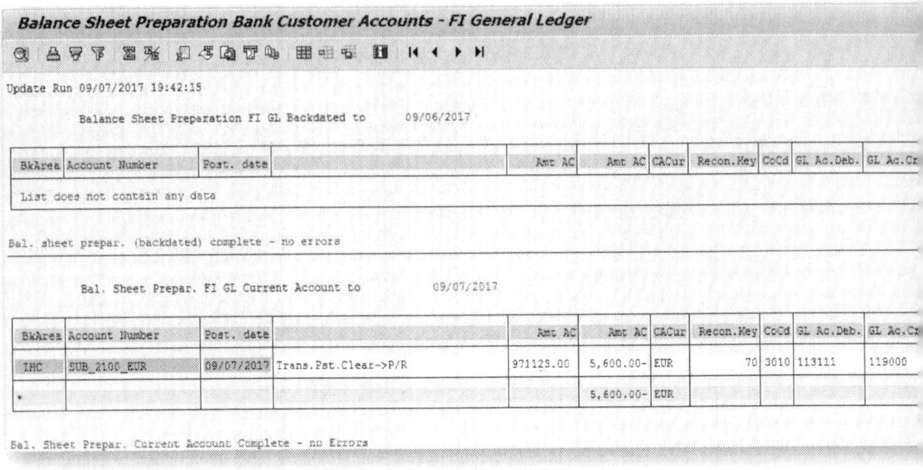

Balance Sheet Preparation Bank Customer Accounts - FI General Ledger

Update Run 09/07/2017 19:42:15

    Balance Sheet Preparation FI GL Backdated to   09/06/2017

BkArea	Account Number	Post. date		Amt AC	Amt AC	CACur	Recon.Key	CoCd	GL Ac.Deb.	GL Ac.Cr
List does not contain any data										

Bal. sheet prepar. (backdated) complete - no errors

    Bal. Sheet Prepar. FI GL Current Account to   09/07/2017

BkArea	Account Number	Post. date		Amt AC	Amt AC	CACur	Recon.Key	CoCd	GL Ac.Deb.	GL Ac.Cr
IHC	SUB_2100_EUR	09/07/2017	Trans.Pst.Clear->P/R	971123.00	5,600.00-	EUR	70	3010	113111	119000
*					5,600.00-	EUR				

Bal. Sheet Prepar. Current Account Complete - no Errors

Figure 5.105: Balance sheet preparation output screen

It should be noted that no actual postings are made during the balance sheet preparation run. The posting is prepared in this step but not made to the SAP general ledger until the FI transfer step.

Step 5: The second step of the two-step process of accounting for the IHC activity is to run the FI transfer step, which consolidates all activity in each IHC account into groups based on several characteristics. Those characteristics include, but are not limited to, the direction of transaction, the posting date, and the offsetting G/L account to be posted to. This step then posts each of these groups of transactions to the IHC EOD Summary Clearing account (113111) on one side and the IHC EOD Technical Clearing account (113009) on the other.

The FI transfer then makes these postings, along with the postings for the balance sheet preparation to the SAP general ledger. The FI transfer step can be run by following the menu path: ACCOUNTING • FINANCIAL SUPPLY CHAIN MANAGEMENT • IN-HOUSE CASH • PERIODIC PROCESSING • GENERAL LEDGER • TRANSFER FI, or by executing transaction code F9HI, as shown in Figure 5.106.

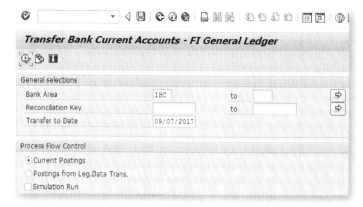

Figure 5.106: FI transfer input screen

After pressing the execute icon ⊕, the postings for both the balance sheet preparation and the FI transfer steps are displayed and made to the SAP general ledger, as shown in Figure 5.107.

Transfer Bank Current Accounts - FI General Ledger

Transfer BCA Accounts - FI GL to   09/07/2017

Update Run   09/07/2017 19:43:35
Transfer Type   FI in Same System as BCA

BkArea	Recon.Key	Post. date	Crcy	G/L	BusA	Value date	Total	D/C
IHC	65	09/07/2017	EUR	113009		09/07/2017	5,600.00	D
IHC	65	09/07/2017	EUR	113110		09/07/2017	5,600.00	D
IHC	65	09/07/2017	EUR	113009		09/07/2017	5,600.00-	C
IHC	65	09/07/2017	EUR	113111		09/07/2017	5,600.00-	C
* Tota	65		EUR				0.00	
*** To	65		EUR				0.00	
IHC	70	09/07/2017	EUR	113111		09/07/2017	5,600.00	D
IHC	70	09/07/2017	EUR	119000		09/07/2017	5,600.00-	C
* Tota	70		EUR				0.00	
*** To	70		EUR				0.00	
**** T			EUR				0.00	

Transfer Fininshed w/o Error

Figure 5.107: FI transfer output screen

Note: the IHC activity is posted to the SAP general ledger through "reconciliation keys". Reconciliation keys summarize the posting data that is posted from SAP subledgers to the SAP general ledger where high volumes of transactions are anticipated, such as for IHC. This means the IHC activity does not post individually to the SAP general ledger. It posts in summarized postings.

To view the postings made from the IHC subledger to the SAP general ledger, follow the menu path: ACCOUNTING • FINANCIAL SUPPLY CHAIN MANAGEMENT • IN-HOUSE CASH • INFORMATION SYSTEM • GENERAL LEDGER TRANSFER • RECONCILIATION BCA / GENERAL LEDGER • LIST OF FI DOCUMENT LINES PER BCA RECONCILIATION KEY, or execute transaction code F97E (see Figure 5.108).

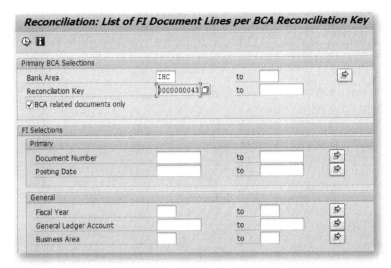

Figure 5.108: View contents of reconciliation key postings

After pressing the execute icon ⊕, the output screen is displayed, as shown in Figure 5.109.

Double-clicking on any of the rows displayed in Figure 5.109 brings up a display, as shown in Figure 5.110.

Reconciliation: List of FI Document Lines per BCA Reconciliation Key

09/06/2017   Reconciliation: FI Document Lines to Recon. Key   Page   1

△	BkArea	Recon.Key	Pstng Date	CoCd	DocumentNo	Itm	G/L	BusA	D/C	Crcy	FI amt doc currency
OOS	IHC	43	07/16/2017	3010	100000024	1	113111		D	EUR	80,000.00
OOS	IHC	43	07/16/2017	3010	100000024	2	119000		D	EUR	89,077.00
OOS	IHC	43	07/16/2017	3010	100000024	3	113111		C	EUR	80,000.00-
OOS	IHC	43	07/16/2017	3010	100000024	4	119000		C	EUR	89,077.00-

Figure 5.109: Reconciliation key postings

Reconciliation: List of FI Document Lines per BCA Reconciliation Key

6/2017   Recon. List: FI Docs/BCa Trans. Postings

oCd	GL Account	BusA	Crcy	Pstng Date	Action Trans.Posting	DocumentNo	Item	D/C	Total	Account Number	Amount in AC
010	119000		EUR	07/16/2017		100000024	4	H	89,077.00-		
010	119000		EUR	07/16/2017	Trans. Clear.->Pays/Recs					SUB_2300_EUR	80,000.00-
010	119000		EUR	07/16/2017	Posting Bal. +/- Change					SUB_2100_EUR	9,077.00-
			EUR						89,077.00-		89,077.00-
010	113111		EUR	07/16/2017		100000024	1	S	80,000.00		
010	113111		EUR	07/16/2017	Trans. Clear.->Pays/Recs					SUB_2300_EUR	80,000.00
			EUR						80,000.00		80,000.00
010	119000		EUR	07/16/2017		100000024	2	S	89,077.00		
010	119000		EUR	07/16/2017	Posting Bal. +/- Change					SUB_2100_EUR	9,077.00
010	119000		EUR	07/16/2017	Trans. Clear.->Pays/Recs					SUB_2100_EUR	80,000.00
			EUR						89,077.00		89,077.00
010	113111		EUR	07/16/2017		100000024	3	H	80,000.00-		
010	113111		EUR	07/16/2017	Trans. Clear.->Pays/Recs					SUB_2100_EUR	80,000.00-
			EUR						80,000.00-		80,000.00-

Figure 5.110: Reformatted reconciliation key postings

Editing current accounts

Business users should minimize the amount of time using the Change Current Accounts program (transaction code F9K2). Instead, the Bank Accounts Display program (transaction code F9K1) should be used. The reason for this is that if someone is editing an IHC current account when the end-of-day process runs, the Start Bank State-Statements program (transaction code F9N1) will fail for that account.

Step 6: The next step is to send bank statements to the IHC account holders. The IHC bank statements are sent for each subsidiary IHC account. The IHC bank statements are sent as FINSTA IDocs. The transaction code F9N1 is used to send all IHC bank statements for one bank area. It is also possible to send bank statements for a single IHC account by following the menu ACCOUNTING • FINANCIAL SUPPLY CHAIN MANAGEMENT • IN-HOUSE CASH • PERIODIC PROCESSING • BANK STATEMENT • NEW RUN • MASS RUN, or by executing the transaction code F9N1 (see Figure 5.111). This program sends a bank statement for any SUB current account that had a transaction on the statement date, assuming the STATEMENTS W/OUT TURNOVERS indicator is not selected. The Create One Single Bank Statement program (transaction code F9N7) sends a bank statement for one current account only. (Note: the internal bank statements are sent only for the SUB current accounts.)

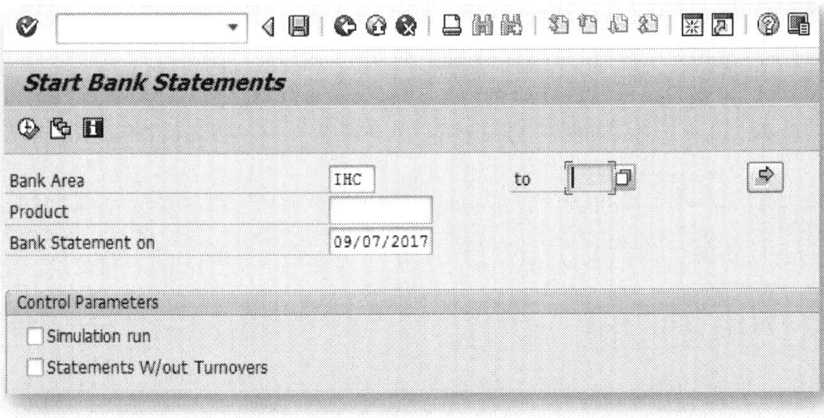

Figure 5.111: Mass send of IHC bank statements

After pressing the execute icon ⊕, a popup message is displayed, as shown in Figure 5.112.

Step 7: The final step in the end-of-day process is to post the bank statements. This is done using transaction code FEBP. The internal bank statements need to be posted to the general ledger for each of the participants. To post the bank statements, follow the menu path: ACCOUNTING • FINANCIAL ACCOUNTING • BANKS • INPUT • BANK STATEMENT • POST, or execute transaction code FEBP (see Figure 5.113 and Figure 6.1).

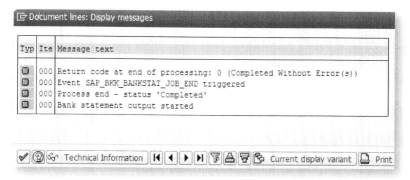

Figure 5.112: Message of successful IHC bank statement send

Update Bank Statement

Bank Statements

			to		
Statement Date			to		
Statement Number			to		
House Bank	IHC		to		
Account ID			to		
Company Code			to		
Currency			to		

Posting Params

- ● Post Immed.
- ○ Generate Batch Input
- ○ Do not post
- ☑ Assign Value Date to Account

☐ Bk Pstg Only
Session Nms 1
☐ Suppress Subsequent Posting

C Man. & Forecast

☐ CM Payment Advice   ☐ Summztn   Planning Type

Algorithms

BELNR Number Interval		to	9999999999	
XBLNR Number Interval	0000000000000000	to	ZZZZZZZZZZZZZZZZ	
Bundling		Items per Bundle	

Output Control

- ☐ Execute as background job
- ☑ Print Bank Statement
- ☑ Print Posting Log
- ☑ Print Statistics

Figure 5.113: Post bank statement input screen

137

Figure 5.114 shows the postings made after executing the Update Bank Statement program.

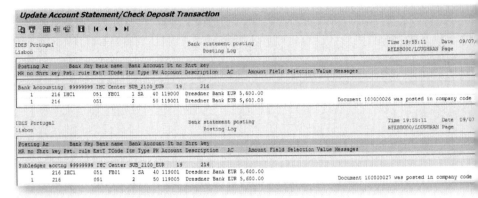

Figure 5.114: Post bank statement output screen

6 IHC accounting entries

This chapter outlines the accounting entries made for the end-to-end scenarios detailed in the previous chapter. The accounting entries are covered by scenario. Since the end-of-day processing steps' accounting entries are covered in each of the other scenarios, end-of-day processing is not included as a separate scenario in this chapter.

6.1 In-House Cash processes

Below are the three IHC processes that are covered in detail in this chapter; the accounting entries for each of them are outlined separately:

▶ Payments on behalf of

▶ Intercompany payments

▶ Centralized incoming payments

To eliminate repetitive content, the accounting entries for manual payment orders will not be outlined. The manual payment orders are a shortened version of the corresponding "payment orders generated automatically" processes.

Table 6.1 is a summary of the G/L accounts used in the example scenario.

Account name	Where defined	G/L account number
IHC EOD Technical Clearing	In-house bank company code	113009
IHC EOD Summary Clearing	In-house bank company code	113111
IHC External Payment Clearing	In-house bank company code	113110

Account name	Where defined	G/L account number
Payment Request Clearing	In-house bank company code	100999
IHC I/C Balance	All company codes	119000
IHC House Bank Clearing	Subsidiary company codes	119001
IHC AR Unapplied Receipts Clearing	Subsidiary company codes	119005

Table 6.1: Summary of G/L accounts used in examples

6.2 Payments on behalf of

In the scenario we covered previously, for payments on behalf of, company code 2100 made a EUR payment to an external vendor through the in-house bank, which is under company code 3010. In this section, the end-to-end accounting entries are outlined.

Step 1: The vendor invoice is entered under company code 2100. The bank details specified are the external vendor's bank details. The payment method entered in the invoice was payment method J, which triggers the payment to be sent to the in-house bank. Below are the accounting entries made when the invoice was entered.

Under company code 2100:

Dr Expense account 449000

   Cr External vendor 50010

Step 2: Next the AP payment program is run under company code 2100. Below are the accounting entries made when the AP payment program was run.

Under company code 2100:

Dr External vendor - 50010

   Cr IHC House Bank Clearing 119001

When the AP payment program is executed, a PAYEXT IDoc is automatically sent to the in-house bank (from the subsidiary), and a payment order is created at the IHB. Once the payment order is posted, a payment request is created.

Step 3: When the Treasury payment program is run at the IHB to pay 2100's external vendor, the following accounting entries are made, and the payment file is sent to the external bank:

Dr IHB External Payment Clearing 113110

    Cr Outgoing Treasury Payments 113401

Step 4: As part of the end-of-day processing, the IHC EOD Technical Clearing account (113009) is used for postings from the in-house bank to the G/L. It is used only for this purpose, and nets to zero at the end of each day.

The net result of the end-of-day postings under company code 3010 for the payment on behalf of is the following:

Dr IHC Balance (trading partner 2100) 119000

    Cr IHC External Payment Clearing 113110

The debit to the 3010/119000 account records the amount subsidiary 2100 owes the IHB. The credit to the 3010/113110 account offsets the debit made to that account when the external payment was executed by the IHB.

Step 5: The in-house bank generates a bank statement to company code 2100. Within the bank statement for the 2100 current account, there is an outgoing payment. When the bank statement posts, the following postings are made:

Dr IHC House Bank Clearing 119001

    Cr IHC Balance Account 119000 (trading partner 3010)

In addition, the debit to the 119001 account clears the posting made to the account when the AP payment program was run.

Step 6: The final postings are made when the in-house bank receives the previous day's bank statement from its external bank, and the following postings are made:

Under company code 3010:

Dr Outgoing Treasury Payments 113401

   Cr External Cash Account 113400

Final: The net result of the above postings is the following, reflecting the balance due to the IHB (see Figure 6.1):

Under company code 2100:

Dr Expense

   Cr IHB Balance account 119000 (trading partner 3010)

Under company code 3010, the following net postings result reflects the amount owed to the IHB by company code 2100:

Dr IHB Balance account (trading partner 2100)

   Cr Cash

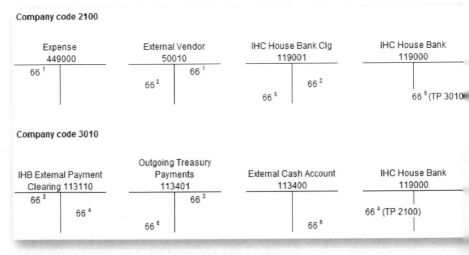

Figure 6.1: Payment on behalf of accounting entries

6.3 Intercompany payments

In the scenario we covered for intercompany payments, company code 2100 made a EUR payment to a subsidiary 2300 through the in-house bank for supplies provided by subsidiary 2300.

The vendor invoice is entered under company code 2100. The bank details specified are the external vendor's bank details. The payment method entered in the invoice was payment method J, which triggers the payment to be sent to the in-house bank. Below are the accounting entries made when the invoice was entered.

Step 1: Customer invoice is entered under company code 2300 for the intercompany receivable from company code 2100. Customer and vendor master records already existed, representing intercompany entities.

Under company code 2300:

Dr I/C AR Customer 2100

   Cr Revenue account

Step 2: Vendor invoice is entered under company code 2100 for the intercompany payable to company code 2300. The vendor bank details specified are to a company code 2300 current account at the in-house bank. Payment method I is used for intercompany payments.

Under company code 2100:

Dr I/C Expenses 165020

   Cr I/C Vendor 2300

Step 3: The AP payment program is run under company code 2100. The payment method used is payment method I, indicating payment should be made through the in-house bank.

Under company code 2100:

Dr I/C Vendor 2300

   Cr IHC House Bank Clearing 119001

When the in-house bank processes the payment from subsidiary 2100, a payment order is automatically created in the IHB. After it is finally posted, it debits the current account of subsidiary 2100 and credits the current account of subsidiary 2300 in the amount of the payment.

Step 4: As part of the end-of-day process, IHC postings are made to the SAP general ledger. In this step, the current balances of the current accounts are made into receivable and payable accounts under 3010.

The net postings from the balance sheet preparation and FI transfer programs are the following:

Dr (Receivables of IHC) IHC I/C Balance (2300) 119000

   Cr (Payables of IHC) IHC I/C Balance (2100) 119000

Step 5: When the in-house bank sends bank statements to the subsidiaries, there is an incoming payment within the bank statement for 2300 current account, and within the bank statement for 2100 current account, there is a corresponding outgoing payment. When the bank statements post, the following postings are made:

Under company code 2300:

Dr IHC I/C Balance 119000

   Cr IHC House Bank Clearing 119001

Posting Area 1

Dr IHC House Bank Clearing 119001

   Cr Customer 2100

Posting Area 2

Under company code 2100:

Dr IHC House Bank Clearing 119001

   Cr IHC I/C Balance 119000

Final: The following are the net results of the above postings, reflecting the balance due to the IHB (see Figure 6.2):

Under company code 2300:

Dr IHB Balance account 119000 (trading partner 3010)
  Cr I/C Revenue

Under company code 2100:

Dr I/C Expense
  Cr IHB Balance account 119000 (trading partner 3010)

Under company code 3010:

Dr (Receivables of IHC) IHC I/C Balance (2300) 119000
  Cr (Payables of IHC) IHC I/C Balance (2100) 119000

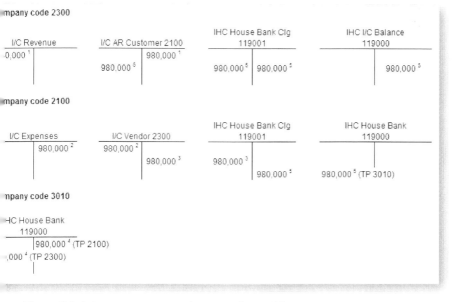

Figure 6.2: Intercompany scenario accounting entries

6.4 Centralized incoming payments

Step 1: The centralized incoming payments scenario starts when the in-house bank receives the previous day's bank statement from its external bank. SAP sees the text in the note to payee field, indicating the payment is for subsidiary 2100, and creates a payment order debiting the IHB clearing partner (EXT_3010_EUR) current account and crediting the SUB_2100_EUR current account. Note: the posting to the IHC External Payment Clearing account is achieved with the use of an EBS search string on the same text as used to create the payment order. The following postings are made under company code 3010:

Dr External house bank main account 113400

   Cr IHC External Payment Clearing 113110

Step 2: As part of the end of day processing, the IHC EOD Technical Clearing account (113009) is used to move the postings from the in-house bank to the G/L. It is used only for this purpose, and nets to zero at the end of each day.

The net result of the end-of-day postings under company code 3010 for the 9,000 EUR payment on behalf of is the following:

Dr 113110 IHC External Payment Clearing

   Cr 119000 IHC I/C Balance (trading partner 2100)

The debit to the 3010/113110 account offsets the credit made to that account when the external bank statement was posted. The credit to the 3010/119000 account records the amount the IHB owes subsidiary 2100.

Step 3: The in-house bank generates a bank statement to company code 2100. Within the bank statement for the 2100 current account, there is an incoming payment. When the bank statement posts, the following postings are made:

Under company code 2100:

Dr IHC I/C Balance 119000 (trading partner 3010)

   Cr IHC House Bank Clearing 119001

Posting Area 1

Dr IHC House Bank Clearing 119001

  Cr IHC AR Unapplied Receipts Clearing 119005

Posting Area 2

Final: The following are the net results of the above postings, reflecting the balance due from the IHB (see Figure 6.3).

Under company code 2100:

Dr IHB Balance account 119000 (trading partner 3010)

  Cr IHC AR Unapplied Receipts/Customer Account

Under company code 3010, the following net postings result, reflecting the amount owed from the IHB to company code 2100.

Dr Cash

  Cr IHB Balance account (trading partner 2100)

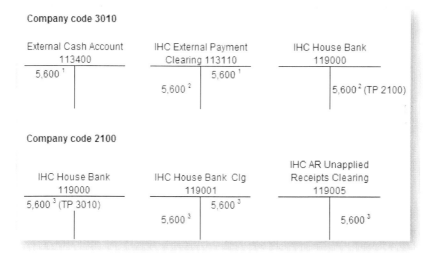

Figure 6.3: Centralized receipt accounting entries

7 IHC subsidiary configuration

The configuration for an SAP IHC implementation can be logically split into configuration for the subsidiaries or company codes that hold accounts at the IHB, and configuration for the IHB(s). We start with the configuration needed for each of the subsidiaries that have a bank account at the IHB, and then in Chapter 8, we cover the configuration of the IHB(s).

The following configuration needs to be done in the subsidiary company codes:

► definition of IHC house bank accounts

► definition of IHC AP payment methods

► F110 configuration for AP IHC payment methods

► IHC internal bank statement configuration

Each of these areas is covered in the following section.

7.1 Definition of the IHC house bank accounts

Define the in-house bank accounts as house bank accounts in each of the subsidiaries' company codes by following the IMG menu: FINANCIAL ACCOUNTING • BANK ACCOUNTING • BANK ACCOUNTS • DEFINE HOUSE BANKS, or by using transaction code FI12. In this step, the subsidiaries' IHC current accounts are created as house bank accounts. In our case, because each subsidiary has one current account at the IHC, there is one IHC house bank account created under each company code. The necessary subsidiary house bank accounts are shown in Table 7.1.

For each of the IHC house bank accounts, the corresponding current accounts need to be created at the IHB. This is covered in Chapter 4 on the IHC master data. The IHC bank key needs to be defined as an EDI partner profile, which is covered in Section 8.5 (ALE configuration).

Company code	Company code name	House bank	Acct ID	Account number	Curr
2100	IDES Portugal	IHC	S-EUR	SUB_2100_EUR	EUR
2300	IDES Spain	IHC	S-EUR	SUB_2300_EUR	EUR
2500	IDES Netherlands	IHC	S-EUR	SUB_2500_EUR	EUR
2900	IDES Sweden	IHC	S-SEK	SUB_2900_SEK	SEK
3000	IDES U.S.	IHC	S-USD	SUB_3000_USD	USD

Table 7.1: Subsidiary IHC house bank accounts

The IHB bank key was defined in the Bank Master Data section of the Master Data chapter, and is used as the BANK KEY for the IHB house bank definitions, and as the EDI PARTNER NUMBER (see Figure 7.1).

In addition to creating the IHB as a house bank, define the EDI partner profile and set the AP IHC payment methods as EDI-compatible payment methods by pressing the EDI COMP. PYT MTHDS button using FI12 (see Figure 7.2).

The G/L account for each of the IHB house bank accounts is 119000, as previously mentioned in Table 4.3 in Chapter 4. For each subsidiary, the balance in the 119000 IHC I/C Balance G/L account represents the amount due to or due from the in-house bank. Figure 7.3 shows the definition of an IHC house bank account in a subsidiary company code.

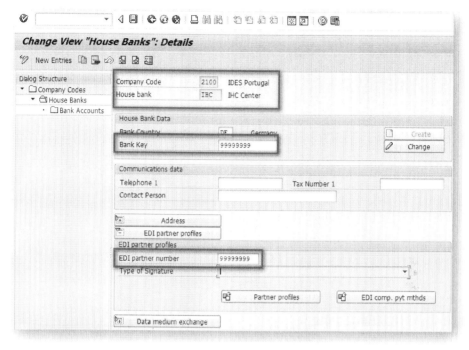

Figure 7.1: Definition of IHC house bank in subsidiary

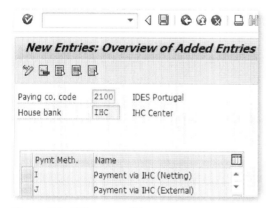

Figure 7.2: EDI-compatible payment methods

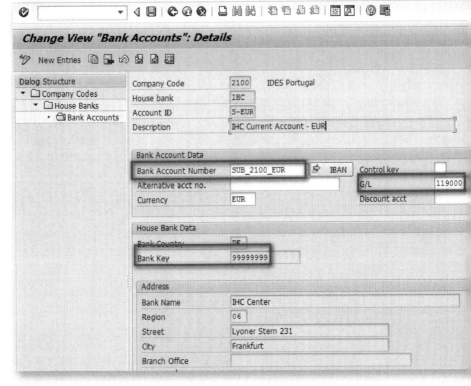

Figure 7.3: Definition of subsidiary's IHC house bank account

7.2 Define AP payment program payment methods

Unique AP payment program payment methods are created, and are only used for IHC processing. For our example scenario, we have defined the following two payment methods:

▶ I – payment via IHC (intercompany netting)

▶ J – payment via IHC (external)

By following the IMG menu path: ACCOUNTING • FINANCIAL ACCOUNTING • BANKS • OUTGOINGS • AUTOMATIC PAYMENT • OPEN ITEMS (CUSTOMERS AND VENDORS), or by using transaction code FBZP, define the IHC AP (F110) payment methods in the required country and company code fields.

The country payment method configuration specifies the general control parameters for a payment method. These fields control or describe the type of payment method, as well as country-specific processing methods that are used by the payment type. In the country-specific settings, select the ACCOUNT NUMBER REQUIRED indicator to ensure an account number is passed in the payment IDoc sent from the subsidiary to the IHB. See Figure 7.4 and Figure 7.5 for the country specific settings.

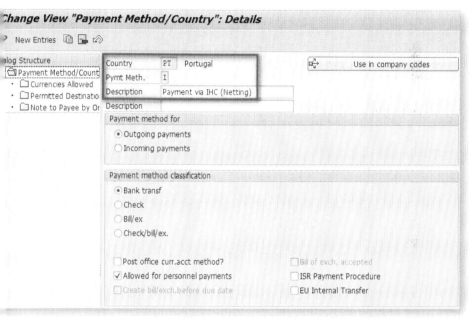

Figure 7.4: Definition of AP payment method at country level (upper half of screen)

Figure 7.5 shows the lower half of the screen from Figure 7.4. For all IHC AP payment methods, a PAYEXT IDoc is the payment medium format. When the AP payment program is run for an IHC payment method, an IDoc containing all the payment information is sent from the subsidiary to the IHB. Therefore, enter RFFOEDI1 as the payment medium program, which generates a PAYEXT IDoc as the payment medium for these two payment methods.

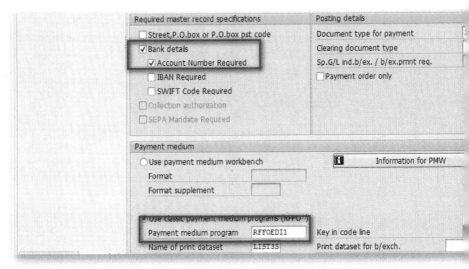

Figure 7.5: Definition of AP payment method at country level (lower half of screen)

In the company-code-specific settings, select FOREIGN BUSINESS PARTNER ALLOWED, FOREIGN CURRENCY ALLOWED, and CUST/VENDOR BANK ABROAD ALLOWED? indicators, assuming these types of payments are included in the project scope, as shown in Figure 7.6.

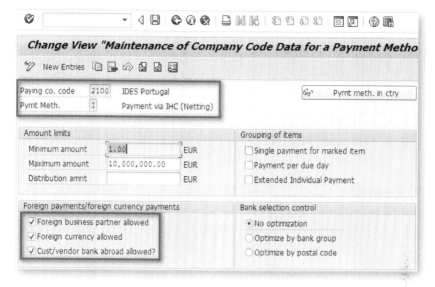

Figure 7.6: Definition of AP payment method at company code level

7.3 Configuration of the AP payment program

In this section, the configuration steps for the AP payment program are covered.

7.3.1 Set up all company codes for payment transactions

The first step is to set up your company code(s) so it/they are available to the payment program. In addition to making the company code available to both the AP and Treasury payment programs, this setting specifies the general control data for the company code. Follow the IMG path: FINANCIAL ACCOUNTING (NEW) • ACCOUNTS RECEIVABLE AND ACCOUNTS PAYABLE • BUSINESS TRANSACTIONS • OUTGOING PAYMENTS • AUTOMATIC OUTGOING PAYMENTS • PAYMENT METHOD/BANK SELECTION FOR PAYMENT PROGRAM • SET UP ALL COMPANY CODES FOR PAYMENT TRANSACTIONS, or go to transaction code FBZP and press the SET UP ALL COMPANY CODES FOR PAYMENT TRANSACTIONS button. The screen in Figure 7.7 is displayed. Make sure each of the subsidiary company codes is populated as shown, with the company's desired settings.

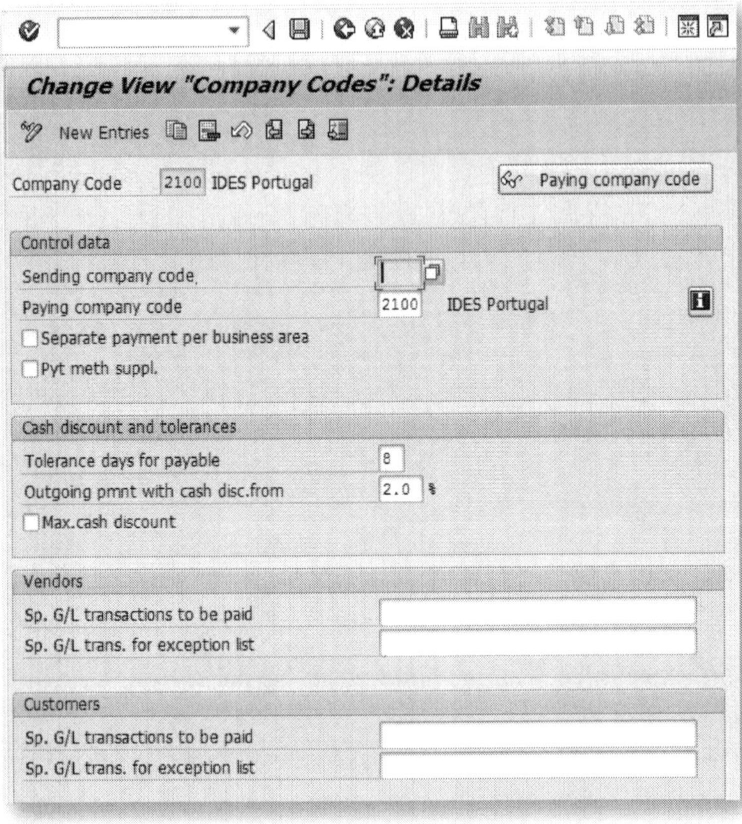

Figure 7.7: Set-up company codes for payment processing

7.3.2 Set up payment company codes for payment transactions

The next step to configuring the AP payment program is to set up parameters for the paying company codes. Do this by following the IMG path: FINANCIAL ACCOUNTING (NEW) • ACCOUNTS RECEIVABLE AND ACCOUNTS PAYABLE • BUSINESS TRANSACTIONS • OUTGOING PAYMENTS • AUTOMATIC OUTGOING PAYMENTS • PAYMENT METHOD/BANK SELECTION FOR PAYMENT PROGRAM • SET UP PAYING COMPANY CODES FOR PAYMENT TRANSACTIONS, or go to transaction code FBZP and press the PAYING COMPANY CODES button. Make sure each of the subsidiary company codes is populated as shown, or with the company's desired settings where relevant. Under the FORMS button make sure the field EDI accompanying sheet form is populated; this is required when creating IDocs as the payment medium format (see Figure 7.8). The field can be populated with an SAP standard form.

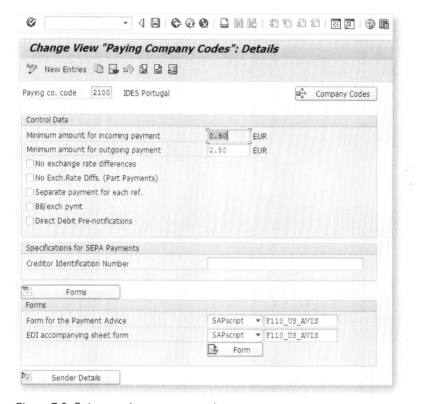

Figure 7.8: Set-up paying company codes

7.3.3   Set up bank determination for payment transactions

To configure the bank determination for the timing of the AP payment program run, follow the IMG path: FINANCIAL ACCOUNTING (NEW) • ACCOUNTS RECEIVABLE AND ACCOUNTS PAYABLE • BUSINESS TRANSACTIONS • OUTGOING PAYMENTS • AUTOMATIC OUTGOING PAYMENTS • PAYMENT METHOD/BANK SELECTION FOR PAYMENT PROGRAM • SET UP BANK DETERMINATION

FOR PAYMENT TRANSACTIONS, or go to transaction code FBZP and press the BANK DETERMINATION button. A screen like the one in Figure 7.9 is shown, which contains several configuration folders on the left (these are explained in detail below), and should be configured for the two AP IHC payment methods, I and J.

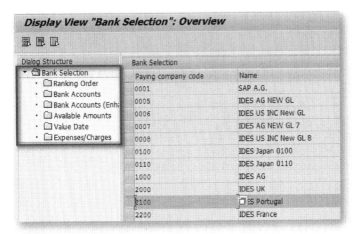

Figure 7.9: Bank determination

Ranking order

The ranking order determines which bank should be selected for the given payment method, as shown in Figure 7.10.

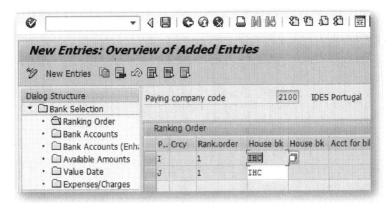

Figure 7.10: Define ranking order for AP IHC payment methods

Bank accounts

Next, for the IHC house bank account and payment method, configure the G/L accounts that are to be posted to when the payment program runs. The account entered here should be the IHC bank clearing account ('1') for both of the IHC AP payment methods, as shown in Figure 7.11.

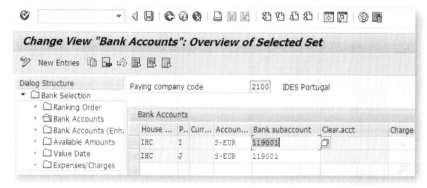

Figure 7.11: Define bank accounts for AP IHC payment methods

Available amounts

Under the AVAILABLE AMOUNT folder, enter the maximum available amount for one payment run, as shown in Figure 7.12.

Figure 7.12: Enter available amounts for IHC account

Value date

The DAYS TO VALUE DATE field allows you to post a payment with a future value date. For the IHC payment methods, there is no value date adjustment, as shown in Figure 7.13. In the AMOUNT LIMIT field, enter the maximum amount of money in the configured bank account that should be available for payment runs.

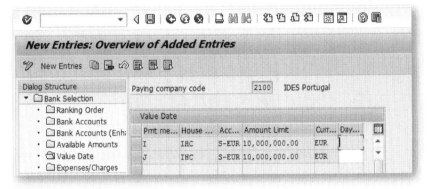

Figure 7.13: Define value date adjustment for AP IHC payment methods

7.3.4   Create RFFOEDI1 variant

After configuration for the payment methods has been done, and before the AP payment program can be run, a payment medium program variant must be defined. The RFFOEDI1 program is what creates the payment IDocs that are sent from the subsidiaries to the in-house bank. The variant created is entered in the AP payment runs on the PRINTOUT/DATA MEDIUM tab. With this variant specified in the AP payment run, the PAYEXT payment IDocs are automatically created in the payment run step, if the CREATE PAYMENT MEDIUM indicator is selected at the payment run pop-up.

To complete this step, execute transaction code SE38, and in the screen that appears, enter the program name RFFOEDI1 in the PROGRAM field, as shown in Figure 7.14.

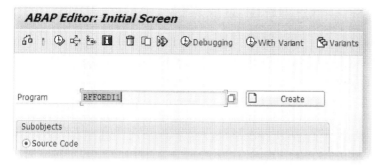

Figure 7.14: Enter program that creates PAYEXT payment IDocs

Press the execute icon ⊕ to define the variant. After entering the IHC PAYMENT METHODS and the in-house bank as the HOUSE BANK, press the save icon 🖫 to save the variant (see Figure 7.15).

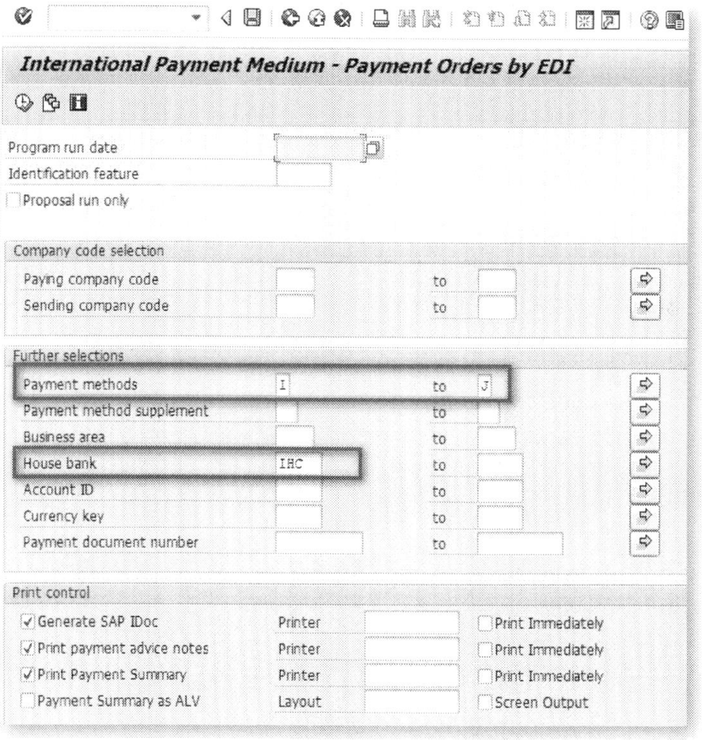

Figure 7.15: Define payment medium program variant

Keep in mind that this variant must be defined on each system as a cut-over step.

7.4 Subsidiary electronic bank statement configuration

The steps followed to configure the internal (IHC) bank statements are the same as those used when configuring external bank statements. The only difference is that the BTC codes configured are not BAI codes from the external banks, but BTC codes defined in the configuration of IHC.

The electronic bank statement (EBS) configuration needs to be configured for both the IHC bank statements sent to the subsidiaries and for the bank statements from the external bank(s) for the external bank accounts used by the IHB. The EBS configuration steps required are the same whether the bank statement is an internally generated bank statement (e.g. one created by IHC), or an external bank statement. Therefore, the configuration steps are covered here only once, using the IHC bank statement as an example.

The electronic bank statement configuration depends on the chart of accounts assigned to the subsidiary company code, which can be found by following the IMG path: FINANCIAL ACCOUNTING • GENERAL LEDGER ACCOUNTING • MASTER DATA • G/L ACCOUNTS • PREPARATIONS • ASSIGN COMPANY CODE TO CHART OF ACCOUNTS.

To configure the electronic bank statement, follow the IMG menu path: FINANCIAL ACCOUNTING (NEW) • BANK ACCOUNTING • BUSINESS TRANSACTIONS • PAYMENT TRANSACTIONS • ELECTRONIC BANK STATEMENT • MAKE GLOBAL SETTINGS FOR ELECTRONIC BANK STATEMENT. After entering the relevant Chart of Accounts in the popup (not shown), the screen in Figure 7.16 is displayed.

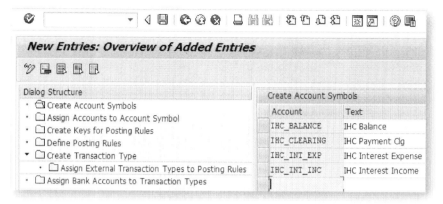

Figure 7.16: Electronic bank statement configuration folders

The electronic bank statement configuration consists of the following steps; each one corresponds to a folder shown in Figure 7.16:

1. Create account symbols that will be used to represent specific general ledger accounts that the electronic bank statements post to.

2. Assign the masked general ledger account number to the symbols created above.

3. Create posting rule keys for each different type of EBS posting that will be made.

4. Define the posting rules for each posting rule key defined above.

5. Create a transaction type that will group all the posting rules to be assigned to a bank account.

6. Assign the business transaction codes to specific posting rules within a transaction type.

7. Finally, assign the bank account to the transaction type.

Next, we will look at each of the steps in detail.

7.4.1 Create account symbols

The first step is to create account symbols that will be used to represent different types of G/L accounts that the IHC bank statements will post to (see again Figure 7.16).

7.4.2 Assign accounts to account symbol

The next step is to assign G/L account numbers to the symbols created in the step above, as shown in Figure 7.17. Typically, these would be masked G/L accounts, but in the case of our example IHC bank accounts, the G/L accounts are the same across all the IHC bank accounts (for example, the IHC I/C Balance account for each IHC house bank account is 119000, and the IHC House Bank Clearing account is 119001, so there is no need to mask the G/L accounts because they are the same for all the IHC bank accounts).

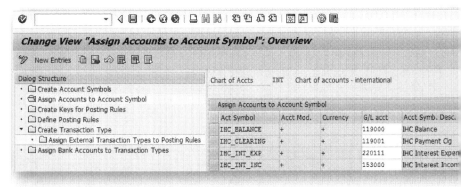

Figure 7.17: Assign G/L accounts to IHC account symbols

7.4.3 Create keys for posting rules

Next, posting rule keys are defined. For each different type of posting rule that is created, define a posting rule key, as shown in Figure 7.18.

164

Naming convention for posting rule and text

It is helpful to use a consistent naming convention for both the posting rule and the associated text. In Figure 7.18, for example, the first two characters of the four-character posting rule indicate that the posting rule relates to IHC bank statements. The second two characters indicate the debit and credit accounts. In the text, describe the debit and credit accounts with abbreviations. This makes the system more maintainable moving forward.

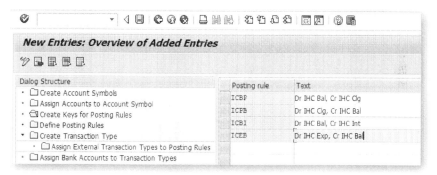

Figure 7.18: Define keys for posting rules

7.4.4 Define posting rules

Next, the details of each posting rule are defined and assigned to the posting rule keys defined above (see Figure 7.19). In this step, the debit and credit accounts are specified, and if the system should clear an offset, an offset is specified.

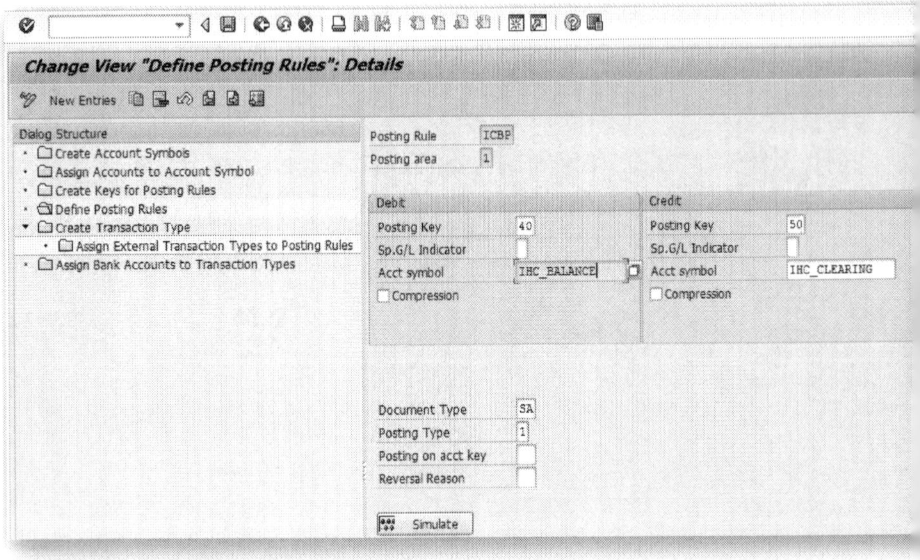

Figure 7.19: Define IHC posting rules

7.4.5 Create transaction type

The next step is to create a transaction type that will group all the posting rules to be assigned to a type of bank account. In our case, there is just one type of bank account – the IHC current accounts. Though there are many different types of bank statement postings for the internal bank statements, only one transaction type is needed, which is called IHC, as shown in Figure 7.20.

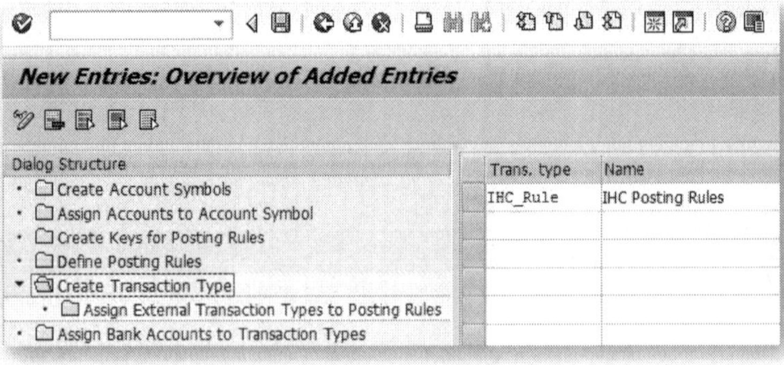

Figure 7.20: Define transaction type for IHC bank accounts

166

7.4.6 Assign external transaction types to posting rules

Next, the posting rules are assigned to BTC codes configured for the IHC transaction type, as shown in Figure 7.21. A payment item transaction type holds the BTC codes, which drives the associated posting rules to be used when the electronic bank statement is posted to the SAP general ledger, see Figure 8.33. The BTC codes to be configured in this step are the BTC codes defined in the DEFINE BUSINESS TRANSACTION CODES IHC configuration step, which is covered in the next chapter.

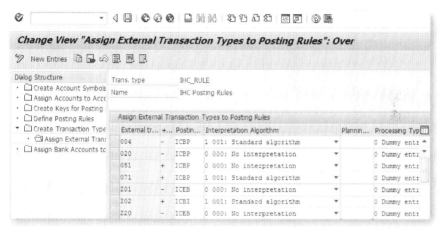

Figure 7.21: Assign posting rules to BTC codes

7.4.7 Assign bank accounts to transaction types

The final step in configuring the IHC electronic bank statements is to assign a transaction type to each bank account. The posting rules defined in that transaction type are then used when the internal bank statement is posted to the SAP general ledger. For the internal bank statement, this step is easy because all the IHC bank accounts are assigned the IHC transaction type, as shown in Figure 7.22.

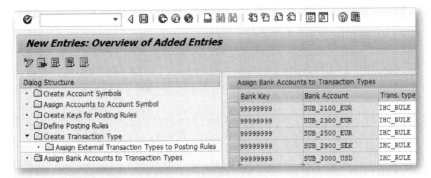

Figure 7.22: Assign transaction type to IHC current accounts

8 IHC configuration

Although there is a significant amount of configuration related to SAP's IHC module, the configuration roughly fits within the following categories:

▶ IHC module specific configuration

▶ Treasury payment program configuration

▶ IHC external bank statement configuration

▶ ALE configuration

The following sections outline the key configuration for each of the above categories.

8.1 IHC module specific configuration

All the SAP IHC module specific configuration related to processing at the IHB can be logically divided into the following categories:

▶ basic settings such as defining the IHB, creating number ranges, business transaction events, etc.

▶ configuration related to IHC master data (The master data are the IHC products, which define the different types of current accounts, and conditions, which fall into the following three categories: interest rates, charges, value dating.)

▶ configuration related to internal and external IHC payment processing

▶ configuration related to centralized receipt IHC payment processing

▶ configuration related to end-of-day processing

8.1.1 IHC basic settings

Define bank area

The central organizational unit in IHC is the BANK AREA, which is defined here. Bank areas require a country and BANK KEY, and are assigned to a COMPANY CODE. For our example scenario, the bank area IHC is defined and assigned to company code 3010. This is the COMPANY CODE that is posted to in the IHC end-of-day process. The postings of the IHB are basically due to/from amounts with the subsidiaries that have current accounts at the IHB. Fields such as language, currency, and calendar are somewhat self-explanatory. Before this configuration can be done, the bank key and GL Variant needs to be defined.

Define and activate the in-house bank, using the IMG customizing path: FINANCIAL SUPPLY CHAIN MANAGEMENT • IN-HOUSE CASH • BASIC SETTINGS • BANK AREA • DEFINE BANK AREA (see Figure 8.1).

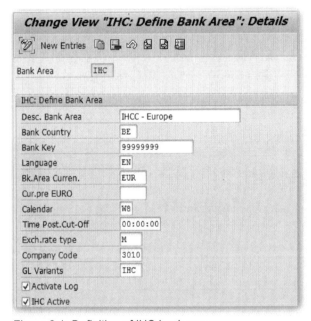

Figure 8.1: Definition of IHC bank area

Define number ranges

In addition to defining the bank areas, this section includes the definition of number ranges, which are listed below.

In this IMG activity, a number range is defined, which are used for IHC logs. Enter 01 as the number range. Create only one number range. Define an interval with at least 1000 numbers. Do not set the indicator for external numbering. To enter the number ranges, follow the IMG path: FINANCIAL SUPPLY CHAIN MANAGEMENT • IN-HOUSE CASH • BASIC SETTINGS • SET UP NUMBER RANGES FOR LOG, and enter the information described above (see Figure 8.2).

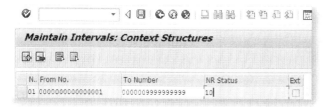

Figure 8.2: Define number range for logs

IHC payment orders are numbered automatically by SAP. In this step, the payment order number ranges are defined by bank area and year. To enter the number ranges, follow the IMG path: FINANCIAL SUPPLY CHAIN MANAGEMENT • IN-HOUSE CASH • BASIC SETTINGS • BANK AREA • SET UP NUMBER RANGES FOR IHC PAYMENT ORDERS (see Figure 8.3).

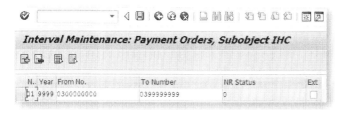

Figure 8.3: Define payment order number range

Next, the number ranges are defined for the current account numbers by bank area. It is best to define the number ranges as alphanumeric current account numbers, as shown in Figure 8.4. This allows for the most flexibility in the current account numbering. To enter the number ranges, follow the IMG path: FINANCIAL SUPPLY CHAIN MANAGEMENT • IN-HOUSE

CASH • BASIC SETTINGS • BANK AREA • MAINTAIN NUMBER RANGES EXT. ACCOUNT NUMBERS.

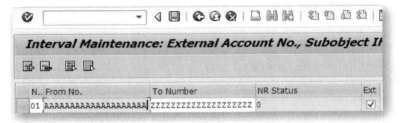

Figure 8.4: Define number ranges for IHC accounts

Set +/- sign postings/GL transfer/name check

The next configuration node can be found by following the IMG path: FINANCIAL SUPPLY CHAIN MANAGEMENT • IN-HOUSE CASH • BASIC SETTINGS • BASIC SETTINGS - POSTINGS • SET +/- SIGN POSTINGS/GL TRANS-FER/NAME CHECK, (see Figure 8.5).

In this section, you can set the +/- sign, which drives how payment amounts are displayed on the IHC programs in SAP. You have the option of displaying a minus sign for IHC credits (incoming payments from the account perspective), as is customary in accounting. Alternatively, you can display a minus sign for debit postings (i.e. outgoing payments).

You can also set how the transfer of the general ledger data to financial accounting is to take place. The TRANS.TYPE FI GEN.LED field specifies if the FI general ledger and Bank Customer Accounts (BCA) are in the same system or in different systems. Note: the Bank Customer Accounts (BCA) is referred to in this book as the IHC subledger.

If selected, the CHECK G/L DATA BEFORE TRANSFER field specifies that the general ledger data should be checked before it is transferred to the general ledger. The system always performs this check in a simulation run. This setting is particularly helpful during testing. This indicator should not be selected if the general ledger is in an external system.

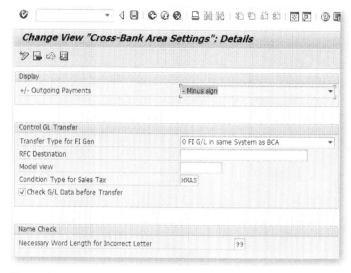

Figure 8.5: Basic settings for the IHC definition

Set texts for incoming/outgoing payments

In this section, you define the displayed abbreviation and the description for outgoing and incoming payments.

Set the description for outgoing and incoming payments to be OUT-FLOW and INFLOW. To enter or change this configuration, follow the path: FINANCIAL SUPPLY CHAIN MANAGEMENT • IN-HOUSE CASH • BASIC SETTINGS • BASIC SETTINGS • POSTINGS • SET TEXTS FOR INCOMING / OUT-GOING PAYMENTS (see Figure 8.6).

Figure 8.6: Define IHC payment flow texts

Activate SAP components

Before the IHC module can be used, it must be activated. This can be done by following the IMG menu path: FINANCIAL SUPPLY CHAIN MANAGEMENT • IN-HOUSE CASH • BASIC SETTINGS • BUSINESS TRANSACTION EVENTS/EVENT CONTROL • ACTIVATE SAP COMPONENTS, and select the check box to the right of IHC (see Figure 8.7).

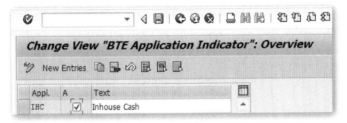

Figure 8.7: Activate the IHC component

Set up business transaction events for SAP in-house cash

There are many Business Transaction Event's (BTE) that need to be defined for the IHC module. These are outlined in the online help in the IMG by following the path: FINANCIAL SUPPLY CHAIN MANAGEMENT • IN-HOUSE CASH • BASIC SETTINGS • BUSINESS TRANSACTION EVENTS/EVENT CONTROL • SET UP BUSINESS TRANSACTION EVENTS FOR SAP IN-HOUSE CASH. These are usually already defined, but make sure that the function modules exist because they will be needed for SAP IHC processing.

8.1.2 Configuration related to IHC master data

In the IHC master data configuration, settings are determined in order to define aspects of conditions, limits, products, and IHC accounts (see Figure 8.8). In this section, we review several key master data configuration settings.

SAP's IHC solution supports three condition group categories that apply to IHB current accounts: interest, charges, and value date activities.

Figure 8.8: IHC master data configuration nodes

The interest and charges conditions apply when account balancing is performed, which is part of the end-of-day process. Interest conditions support the functionality to charge interest on debit (negative) balances and give interest on credit balances. Charge-related conditions allow the IHB to charge the subsidiaries for specific transactions; e.g. to charge for wire transfers over low-value payment methods such as ACH or SEPA.

The logic of how the conditions are assigned to the IHC current accounts is as follows:

▶ Condition groups are assigned to condition areas.

▶ Condition areas are assigned to products.

▶ Products are assigned to current accounts.

▶ Products are assigned to in-house banks.

▶ Current accounts are the bank accounts at the in-house bank.

Enter basic settings for conditions

Before doing other condition-related configuration, enter the ENTER BASIC SETTINGS FOR CONDITIONS configuration. Here, the following settings apply to all conditions in the client:

▶ Dual control for changes to conditions. This means that after creating a condition or changing a condition, it must be approved or released by a different user to the one who made the change, before it can be used.

▶ Specify whether conditions should be time-dependent.

▶ Specify how capital yield tax is to be processed in the account balancing step.

To enter the configuration, follow the IMG menu path: FINANCIAL SUPPLY CHAIN MANAGEMENT • IN-HOUSE CASH • MASTER DATA • CONDITIONS • ENTER BASIC SETTINGS FOR CONDITIONS (see Figure 8.9).

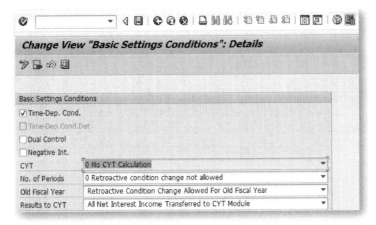

Figure 8.9: Enter basic settings for conditions

Conditions are created with respect to a condition area that is later assigned to a product. One condition area can be assigned to several products. When an IHC account is created, it is defined with a specific product. The product drives the functionality of the IHC account.

Setup condition areas

To define a condition area, follow the IMG path: FINANCIAL SUPPLY CHAIN MANAGEMENT • IN-HOUSE CASH • MASTER DATA • CONDITIONS • SETUP CONDITION AREAS (see Figure 8.10).

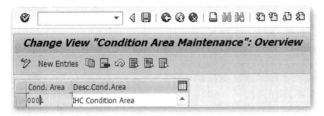

Figure 8.10: Define condition area

Define condition categories

CONDITION CATEGORIES determine the basic functionality of a condition. They are divided into three condition group categories: interest, charge, and value date, and are the three types of conditions supported by SAP's IHC module. Condition categories determine the basic functionality of the condition. Each condition category is of a specific condition class: balancing conditions (11), transaction conditions (12), and value date conditions (13).

It is important to understand the conditions that are delivered with SAP standard, because these can be more easily used in an IHC implementation and are most likely all that are required. Table 8.1 shows the condition categories delivered with standard SAP, which can be viewed by following the IMG path: FINANCIAL SUPPLY CHAIN MANAGEMENT • IN-HOUSE CASH • MASTER DATA • CONDITIONS • DEFINE CONDITION CATEGORIES.

Condition group category	Condition category
Interest (1)	Debit interest (0001)
	Credit interest (0002)
	Loan overdraft interest (0003)
	Transaction interest (0004)
	Commitment interest (0013)
	Interest penalty (0014)
Charges (2)	Transaction charges (0005)
	Item charges (0006)
	Dispatch charges (0007)
	Account maintenance charge (0008)
	Direct charge (0012)
Value date (3)	Value date (0010)
	Subject to final value date (0011)

Table 8.1: Condition categories delivered with SAP

Assign differentiation types to condition categories

Differentiation types help sub-divide condition categories, enabling creation of more complex conditions and functionality. It is possible to make changes to the SAP-delivered settings; for example, it is possible to differentiate the transaction charges as charges for a debit transfer versus a credit transfer. The standard SAP differentiation types available for use are:

▶ Payment item transaction type

▶ Medium

▶ Item counter

▶ Dispatch expense counter

▶ Transaction type category

▶ Feature

▶ Activity

▶ Second transaction type category

▶ Position type

The available differentiation types can be assigned to all condition categories. To restrict the preliminary selection of differentiation types for a condition category, you must assign the useable differentiation types to each condition category. This restricts which differentiation types are displayed when you select the differentiation. The allocation of the differentiation types is done separately for each condition area. To view the SAP-delivered condition categories, follow the configuration path: FINANCIAL SUPPLY CHAIN MANAGEMENT • IN-HOUSE CASH • MASTER DATA • CONDITIONS • DIFFERENTIATION TYPES • ASSIGN DIFFERENTIATION TYPES TO CONDITION CATEGORIES (see Figure 8.11).

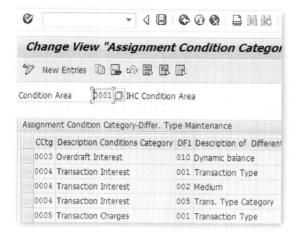

Figure 8.11: Assign differentiation types to condition categories

Setup prefix

The prefix is used by SAP to differentiate attributes and products config-uration used for a specific IHC implementation. Each system should have its own prefix to ensure that newly created attributes and products do not overwrite existing ones.

It is not possible to save IHC attributes and products without first specify-ing a prefix.

The internal key for attributes and products is generated automatically. It consists of a prefix of up to 10 characters, and a consecutive number. The prefix is not saved to a transport, and therefore needs to be created in each system. The prefix is maintained by following the configuration path: FINANCIAL SUPPLY CHAIN MANAGEMENT • IN-HOUSE CASH • MASTER DATA • PRODUCT DEFINITION • SET UP PREFIX (see Figure 8.12).

Maintenance of Prefix for Key Fields	
Prefix for Key Fields	ZIHC

Figure 8.12: Definition of system prefix

Create product

When you create an IHC current account, you assign a product. The product drives the functionality of the account; e.g. if and how interest is charged on account balances, characteristics of different account balancing, or which payment methods can be used for the account. Therefore, within the product definition, you determine whether account balancing is to be done, whether bank statements are to be sent, whether interest is to be charged, etc. You also set the types of transactions/payments that can be made from the account; for example, only wire transfers are allowed for one type of account, but for another type of account, wires, low-value (SEPA, ACH), and checks are allowed.

The product also controls the screen sequence and display of an account's attributes. When creating an IHC current account, only products that are both active and within the validity period can be used.

Products are defined by following the configuration menu path: FINANCIAL SUPPLY CHAIN MANAGEMENT • IN-HOUSE CASH • MASTER DATA • PRODUCT DEFINITION • CREATE PRODUCT (see Figure 8.13). The product should be given a name in the description field. The system is more flexible if the VALID FROM date is back-dated and the VALID TO field is set to 12/31/9999.

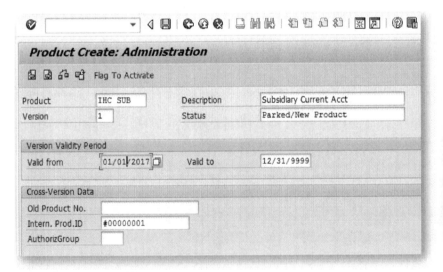

Figure 8.13: Create IHC account product

The products are maintained by using the product configurator delivered with IHC. The user selects the features and characteristics of each product. As part of our example scenario, the following products should be configured:

▶ CPD – Creating this product is an SAP requirement.

▶ SUB – This product is to be used for the IHC subsidiary internal bank accounts with the IHB.

▶ EXT – Use this product to record IHC activity executed between the In-house Bank and the external bank accounts.

Several screens appear, one after the other, with attribute trees, as shown in Figure 8.14. On these screens, you assign the attributes. On each screen, a traffic light is displayed for every attribute, showing whether an attribute was activated or not. The attributes are activated by selecting the traffic lights.

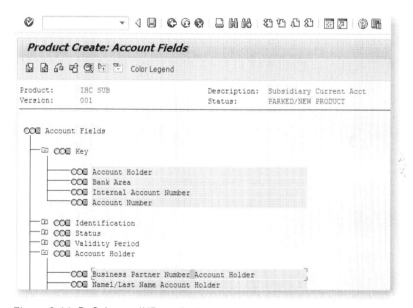

Figure 8.14: Defining an IHB product

With the 'Detail' icon it is possible to define the details of an attribute. Depending on the attribute, the detail is displayed which drives the processing for that attribute. In Figure 8.15, for example, the detail screen for the BUSINESS PARTNER NUMBER ACCOUNT HOLDER field is displayed.

181

Here, this field is set as "required" because an IHC current account should not be created unless it has an assigned business partner with the role of ACCOUNT HOLDER assigned.

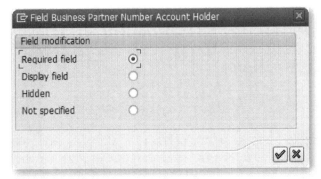

Figure 8.15: Attribute detail

Once the product is defined, click on the FLAG TO ACTIVATE button to activate the product, see Figure 8.15.

Assign products to bank areas

Products are assigned to a bank area by following the configuration menu path: FINANCIAL SUPPLY CHAIN MANAGEMENT • IN-HOUSE CASH • MASTER DATA • PRODUCT DEFINITION • ASSIGN PRODUCTS TO BANK AREAS (see Figure 8.16).

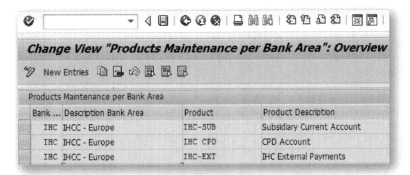

Figure 8.16: Assign products to bank area

Maintain formats for bank statements

In typical IHC implementations, the FINSTA IDoc format is used for the IHC (internal) bank statements in most cases. The FINSTA IDoc format is usually set as the default format for the IHC account holder. However, there are some instances when a subsidiary is not in SAP but still participates in the IHC, in which case a custom bank statement type should be defined. The formats for the IHC (internal) bank statements are defined by following the configuration path: FINANCIAL SUPPLY CHAIN MANAGEMENT • IN-HOUSE CASH • MASTER DATA • ACCOUNT • MAINTAIN FORMATS FOR BANK STATEMENTS (see Figure 8.17).

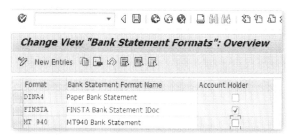

Figure 8.17: IHC bank statement formats

Maintain dispatch type for bank statements

The Application Link Enabling (ALE) dispatch types are defined by following the configuration path: FINANCIAL SUPPLY CHAIN MANAGEMENT • IN-HOUSE CASH • MASTER DATA • ACCOUNT • MAINTAIN DISPATCH TYPE FOR BANK STATEMENTS (see Figure 8.18). The ALE dispatch type is usually also set as the default dispatch type for the account holder. As mentioned previously, there are times when a subsidiary is not in SAP but is still able to participate in the IHC functionality.

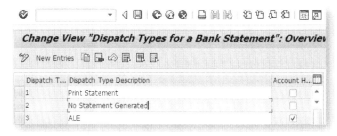

Figure 8.18: IHC dispatch types

8.1.3 IHC payment processing configuration

There are two "processes" in SAP's IHC solution – payment and periodic. The payment process relates to payment processing. The periodic process relates to the end-of-day process. Refer to Chapters 3 and 5 for more information on each of these processes.

Define transaction types

The first step in the configuration of IHC payment processing configuration is to define the types of payment orders that will be used in the IHB being implemented. These are the different types of payments that are needed at the IHB. These transaction types are bank-area independent. For each transaction type, enter a ten-character name for the transaction type, and a description, and select the Ext. indicator if the transaction type corresponds to a payment order that generates an external payment.

Design before configuration

 Before getting started on the IHC configuration, it is advisable to know in advance the types of payment orders the IHB should support. Understanding the configuration is easier when the scenarios have been sufficiently thought through. Please see Table 2.2 for the payment order types used in this book.

To define TRANSACTION TYPES, follow the configuration path: FINANCIAL SUPPLY CHAIN MANAGEMENT • IN-HOUSE CASH • ACCOUNT MANAGEMENT • PAYMENT PROCESSES IN IN-HOUSE CASH • DEFINE TRANSACTION TYPES (see Figure 8.19).

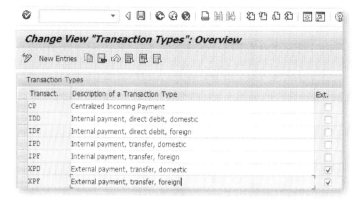

Figure 8.19: Define transaction types

Define clearing partner

In this configuration activity, you set up clearing partners to which you will forward external payment orders.

All payment orders for external recipients (the recipient's account is not in the same bank area as the payer of the payment order) are forwarded to a clearing partner. The external recipient could be an external bank or another BANK AREA. If the clearing partner is an external bank, the type should be set to FI. If the external recipient is another Bank Area, the type should be set to IHC.

To define CLEARING PARTNERS, follow the configuration path: FINANCIAL SUPPLY CHAIN MANAGEMENT • IN-HOUSE CASH • ACCOUNT MANAGEMENT • PAYMENT PROCESSES IN IN-HOUSE CASH • DEFINE CLEARING PARTNER (see Figure 8.20).

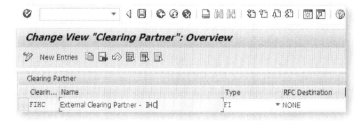

Figure 8.20: Define external clearing partner

Define transaction type for automatic payments

In the next configuration node, mapping is completed to enable SAP to derive a payment order transaction type based on the in-house bank, the AP payment method, the currency of the payment, and the recipient's bank country from the PAYEXT IDoc sent from the subsidiary, as shown in Figure 8.21. This configuration node is found under: FINANCIAL SUPPLY CHAIN MANAGEMENT • IN-HOUSE CASH • ACCOUNT MANAGEMENT • PAYMENT PROCESSES IN IN-HOUSE CASH • DEFINE TRANSACTION TYPE FOR AUTOMATIC PAYMENTS.

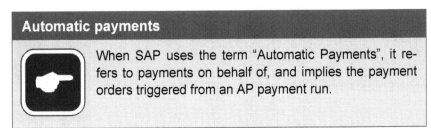

Automatic payments

When SAP uses the term "Automatic Payments", it refers to payments on behalf of, and implies the payment orders triggered from an AP payment run.

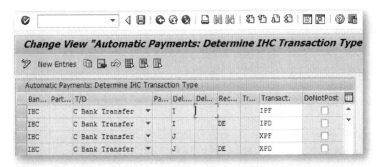

Figure 8.21: Map from AP payment method to payment order transaction type

Make basic settings for payment processes

Next, the main IHC payment processing configuration is defined by bank area. This configuration consists of several configuration steps, and can be found by following the path: FINANCIAL SUPPLY CHAIN MANAGEMENT • IN-HOUSE CASH • ACCOUNT MANAGEMENT • PAYMENT PROCESSES IN IN-HOUSE CASH • MAKE BASIC SETTINGS FOR PAYMENT PROCESSES. We will now walk through each of the folders in this configuration node.

▶ Processing Transaction Types in Bank Area

Here, you specify which transaction types are allowed in a bank area and how they should be posted. If a transaction type is not available here for a bank area, it cannot be used for a payment order created in the bank area (see Figure 8.22).

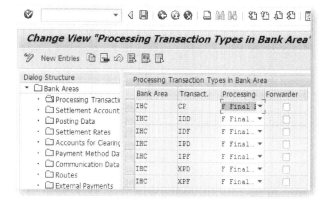

Figure 8.22: Define transaction types for bank area

▶ SETTLEMENT ACCOUNTS

In this step, the following are defined:

  ▶ current accounts for provisional postings

  ▶ settlement accounts for provisional and final postings

Note that the entries for final postings are only allowed in combination with the settlement posting type.

The transaction type and business partner fields are optional. Populating the transaction type and business partner fields further differentiates between the accounts that are to be posted to. If the transaction type is populated, ensure that the credit/debit indicator corresponds to the transaction type attributes.

Always define the settlement and provisional accounts in the currency of the current accounts that will ultimately be posted to, as shown in Figure 8.23.

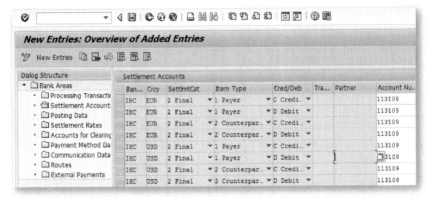

Figure 8.23: Define settlement accounts POSTING DATA

In this configuration, we define the posting parameters that SAP uses to post the current accounts, and which drive the accounting entries, as shown in Figure 8.24.

Configuration tip

Make sure the transaction type and the credit/debit indicator are aligned.

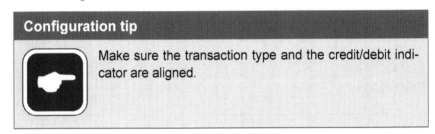

Figure 8.24: Define the payment item transaction types

▶ SETTLEMENT RATES

In the case of a currency conversion, the exchange rate type entered here (see Figure 8.25) is used to calculate the amounts for posting to the current accounts, and the settlement amounts for posting. If there is a currency conversion for debit items, the selling rate is transferred; the buying rate is transferred if the currency is converted for a credit item.

The clearing partner field is optional. In the case of external payments, you can use this field to define exchange rate types based on the clearing partner, if desired.

Figure 8.25: Define the exchange rate type to be used for IHC postings

▶ ACCOUNT FOR CLEARING PARTNER

Enter current accounts for each clearing partner for clearing payment orders that have been created at the IHB, as shown in Figure 8.26. Postings are made to these offsetting accounts when payment orders are forwarded to a clearing partner, as in the case of external IHB payments.

Offsetting accounts must be created for each clearing partner and currency in which payment orders will be forwarded to the clearing partner. You can also define different accounts for the different settlement categories.

189

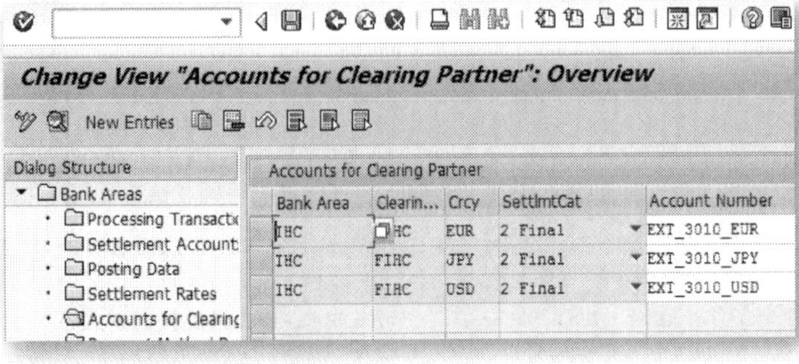

Figure 8.26: Define IHC accounts for clearing partners

▶ PAYMENT METHOD DATA

Here, you define the payment methods which will be contained in the outbound IDoc from the in-house bank to the determined clearing partner, and which will be used for the payment request created. The derived payment method and payment method supplement are determined by the in-house bank, the clearing partner, the currency of the payment to the receiving bank's country, the payment order transaction type, the delivered payment method, and the delivered payment method supplement (see Figure 8.27). .

This key configuration is used to drive whether a payment should be sent using a low-value local payment method or a cross-border payment method, based on the receiving bank country field; for example, if the payment is a USD payment and the receiving bank country is the U.S., the payment method is set to 2 – low-value payment. The payment is then sent as an ACH payment from the IHB's USD account, which is domiciled in the U.S.

If no entry is determined based on the outbound payment's data, the system forwards the original payment method and payment method supplement contained in the inbound IDoc from the subsidiary.

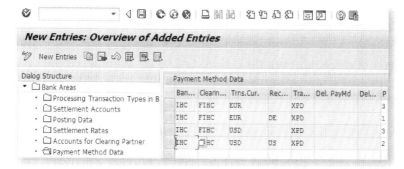

Figure 8.27: Define payment method for external payments

▶ COMMUNICATION DATA

This configuration contains the parameters for communication between an IDoc and a clearing partner. For each currency in which the payment order will be forwarded to a clearing partner, define the following parameters, as shown in Figure 8.28:

▶ partner type of the recipient

▶ partner number of the recipient

▶ message code

▶ message function

When the subsequent outbound IDoc is generated, these values are transferred to the control record. They are required in order to send the IDoc and to ensure correct inbound processing in the recipient system. The message code and message function fields are optional, and their values are freely definable. However, they must correspond to the entries in the partner profile definition which apply to inbound IDocs in the recipient system. This determines whether the recipient should process the inbound IDoc as an incoming IHC payment for cross-bank-area payments (process code PEXN), or as an incoming FI payment for external payments with payment program F111 (process code PEXC).

In addition, the following account details are written to the outbound IDoc as the sender bank details and are used to identify the sender in the recipient system:

▶ bank country

- ▶ bank key
- ▶ account number

To carry out cross-bank-area payments, a sender account must be entered here in the recipient's SAP In-House Cash component. This account must correspond to an account in the current account system of the recipient IHC bank area.

To carry out external payments in the FI subsystem of the recipient, account details must be entered here to identify the sender when the Inbound IDoc is processed in the recipient system.

To identify the IDoc sender and process the IDoc in the recipient system, the account must correspond to the account details of the clearing partner entered in the recipient system for processing inbound IDocs. You can find the account details in the SET UP CREATION OF PAYMENT REQUESTS FOR INBOUND IDoc configuration. The bank details entered are only used for internal identification.

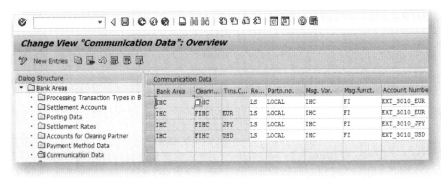

Figure 8.28: Enter communication data

▶ ROUTES

Enter the clearing partner the system should forward an external or cross-bank-area payment order to. In our example, the only clearing partner is for external payments, as defined in Figure 8.29.

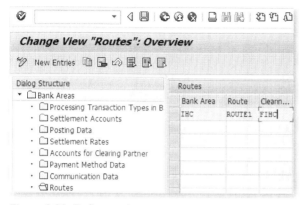

Figure 8.29: Define routes

▶ EXTERNAL PAYMENTS

Specify which clearing accounts are to be used to make external pay-ments for each BANK AREA by currency and transaction type, as shown in Figure 8.30.

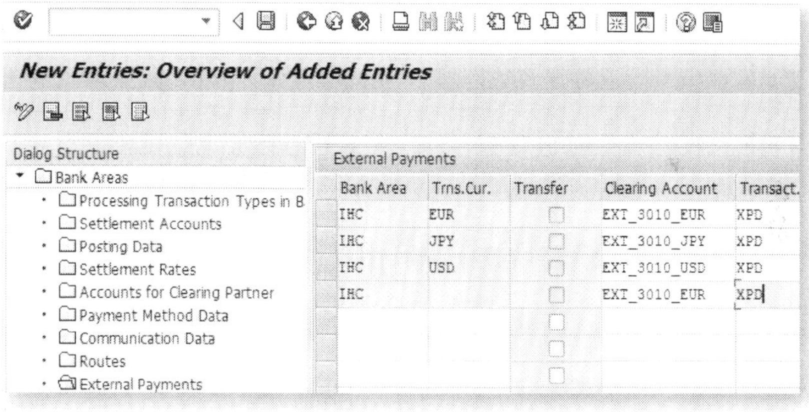

Bank Area	Trns.Cur.	Transfer	Clearing Account	Transact.
IHC	EUR	☐	EXT_3010_EUR	XPD
IHC	JPY	☐	EXT_3010_JPY	XPD
IHC	USD	☐	EXT_3010_USD	XPD
IHC		☐	EXT_3010_EUR	XPD
		☐		
		☐		
		☐		

Figure 8.30: Define clearing accounts for external payments

Define default setting for transaction type

In this next step, we define the IHC payment order transaction type that should be the default setting for each of the five different transactions for creating IHC payment orders. The five types of transactions are: internal, external, bank transfer, debit memo, and expert mode.

To specify the default setting for transaction types, follow the configuration menu path: FINANCIAL SUPPLY CHAIN MANAGEMENT • IN-HOUSE CASH • ACCOUNT MANAGEMENT • PAYMENT PROCESSES IN IN-HOUSE CASH • DEFINE DEFAULT SETTING FOR TRANSACTION TYPE (see Figure 8.31).

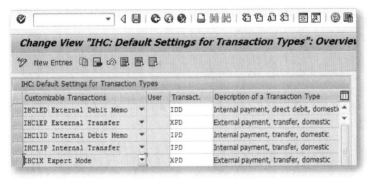

Figure 8.31: Define the default payment order transaction types

Define business transaction codes

In this configuration, the types of transactions/payments that can be sent through the different types of accounts are defined. For each type of transaction, the BUSINESS TRANSACTION CODE (BTC) that will be used to note this type of transaction in the bank statement is specified. The BTC code is a three-digit code that designates a specific type of bank statement transaction, and is comparable to a BAI code in BAI formatted bank statements. In the same way configuration is done in SAP for external bank statements, posting rules for each BTC code are also defined.

A payment order has a payment order transaction type, which defines the type of transaction it is; e.g. bank charge, interest charge, wire payment, etc. Each payment order transaction type is composed of two payment item transaction types. The payment item transaction types are like an accounting entry debit and credit. For each payment item transaction type, you specify the offsetting entry. It is possible to have more than one offsetting entry, in which case the system will prompt for it.

The IHC business transaction codes are three-character alphanumeric codes. BUSINESS TRANSACTION CODES (BTCs) are codes that distinguish transactions in bank statements. SAP is delivered with some pre-set BTCs. Alternatively, new BTCs can also be defined. If new BTCs are defined, it is important to use a consistent naming convention for them. BTCs are defined by following the configuration menu path: FINANCIAL SUPPLY CHAIN MANAGEMENT • IN-HOUSE CASH • ACCOUNT MANAGEMENT • BASIC FUNCTIONS IN ACCOUNT MANAGEMENT • DEFINE BUSINESS TRANSACTION CODES (see Figure 8.32).

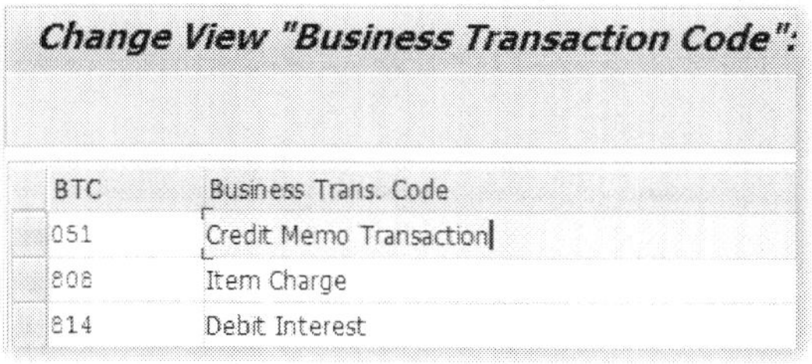

BTC	Business Trans. Code
051	Credit Memo Transaction
808	Item Charge
814	Debit Interest

Change View "Business Transaction Code":

Figure 8.32: Define business transaction codes

Maintain transaction types

In the next step, the BTC codes are assigned to payment item transaction types by following the configuration IMG menu path: FINANCIAL SUPPLY CHAIN MANAGEMENT • IN-HOUSE CASH • ACCOUNT MANAGEMENT • BASIC FUNCTIONS IN ACCOUNT MANAGEMENT • MAINTAIN TRANSACTION TYPES (see Figure 8.33).

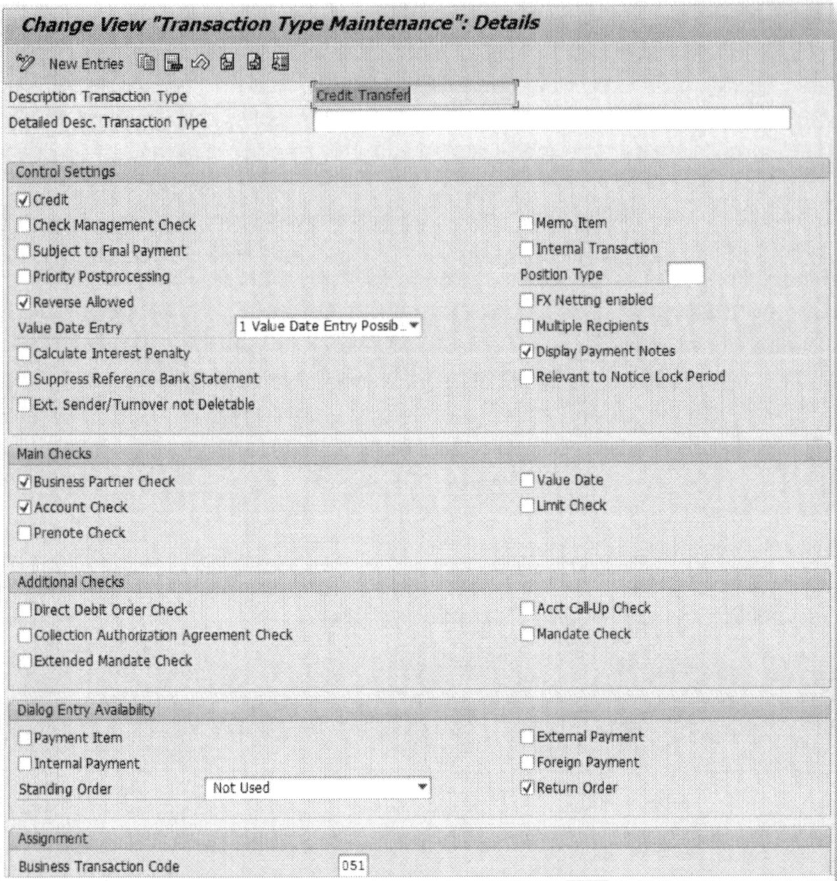

Figure 8.33: Definition of a payment item transaction type

Assign offsetting transaction types

Next, for each payment item transaction type, a corresponding offsetting transaction type is assigned.

Offsetting transaction types are the corresponding transaction types for the second payment item of the payment order. When an internally generated payment order is created, the transaction type for the second item is automatically assigned based on the transaction type of the first item, which is driven by this configuration. For each TRANSACTION TYPE, it is possible to assign several offsetting transaction types; and if multiple offsetting transaction types are assigned, the user must select one of the offsetting transaction types entered here.

To assign the offsetting transaction type, follow the configuration menu path: FINANCIAL SUPPLY CHAIN MANAGEMENT • IN-HOUSE CASH • ACCOUNT MANAGEMENT • BASIC FUNCTIONS IN ACCOUNT MANAGEMENT • ASSIGN OFF-SETTING TRANSACTION TYPES (see Figure 8.34).

Figure 8.34: Define offsetting transaction types

Maintain accounts for payment transactions

Clearing accounts are required in the case of errored payment transactions. The following two types of accounts must be specified by bank area and currency combination:

▶ One-time account

  ▶ This is used if, with an externally initiated payment transaction, no recipient account or turnover item account can be identified, or if the account is blocked.

  ▶ This is used if the item is diverted to CPD during post processing.

▶ Clearing account

  ▶ This is used for transaction charges and transaction interest that cannot be charged to the recipient (e.g. for returns), and for guaranteed amounts for which the bank is liable if a check is returned.

197

A single CPD technical clearing account current account is required for each bank area and each functional currency of the bank area owner. We assign the same CPD technical account to both types of accounts in this configuration step. For more information on this CPD account, see Chapter 4 and Table 4.2.

To assign the accounts, follow the configuration menu path: FINANCIAL SUPPLY CHAIN MANAGEMENT • IN-HOUSE CASH • ACCOUNT MANAGEMENT • MAINTAIN ACCOUNTS FOR PAYMENT TRANSACTIONS (see Figure 8.35).

Change View "Maintain Accounts for Payment Transactions":

New Entries

Bank	Currency	One-Time Account	Clearing Account	
IHC	EUR	CPD	CPD	
IHC	JPY	CPD	CPD	
IHC	USD	CPD	CPD	

Figure 8.35: Assign the SAP required CPD accounts

We will now walk through a few required configuration steps for centralized incoming payments, which can be found under the following configuration menu node: FINANCIAL SUPPLY CHAIN MANAGEMENT • IN-HOUSE CASH • ACCOUNT MANAGEMENT • PAYMENT PROCESSES IN IN-HOUSE CASH • CENTRAL CASH RECEIPT / INCOMING BANK STATEMENTS.

IHC account determination from payment notes

In this configuration, the search string that drives the payment order to a specific current account is specified. In our case, the search string is COMP2100. If this text is in the note to payee field of a bank statement transaction, SAP creates a payment order that will debit the external payment clearing account and credit the SUB_2100_EUR current account. To get to the configuration, follow the configuration menu path: FINANCIAL SUPPLY CHAIN MANAGEMENT • IN-HOUSE CASH • ACCOUNT MANAGEMENT • PAYMENT PROCESSES IN IN-HOUSE CASH • CENTRAL CASH RECEIPT / INCOMING BANK STATEMENTS • IHC ACCOUNT DETERMINATION FROM PAYMENT NOTES. The configuration is shown in Figure 8.36.

Figure 8.36: ROBO search string text specified

Set up account determination for incoming payment

The next configuration node is found by following the configuration menu path: FINANCIAL SUPPLY CHAIN MANAGEMENT • IN-HOUSE CASH • ACCOUNT MANAGEMENT • PAYMENT PROCESSES IN IN-HOUSE CASH • CENTRAL CASH RECEIPT / INCOMING BANK STATEMENTS • SET UP ACCOUNT DETERMINATION FOR INCOMING PAYMENT.

In this configuration, we specify the current account corresponding to the house bank account that the bank statement relates to. The current account for incoming payments, where the system is unable to determine a recipient account, is specified (see Figure 8.37).

Figure 8.37: Map house bank account to EXT account for incoming payments

In the next configuration step, the external BTC codes (similar to BAI codes) that could trigger an incoming payment order creation are specified. If any BTC code should trigger an incoming payment order creation, the EXTERNAL TRANSACTION field can be left blank. Specify if a debit or credit memo payment order should be created using the CRED/DEB field. Lastly, in the TRANSACTION TYPE field, the payment order transaction type is specified. The payment order created will have this payment order transaction type. Enter this data by following the configuration menu path: FINANCIAL SUPPLY CHAIN MANAGEMENT • IN-HOUSE CASH • ACCOUNT MANAGEMENT • PAYMENT PROCESSES IN IN-HOUSE CASH • CENTRAL CASH

RECEIPT / INCOMING BANK STATEMENTS • DEFINE TRANSACTION TYPES FOR INCOMING PAYMENT (see Figure 8.38).

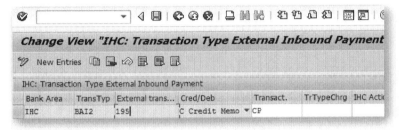

Figure 8.38: Define payment order transaction type

8.1.4 IHC end-of-day processing configuration

Having described the configuration related to the payment process, we'll now move on to the configuration related to the periodic or end-of-day process.

As part of the end-of-day process, the IHC current account activity is posted to the ledger. We will now cover the key configuration nodes related to posting the IHC activity to the SAP general ledger.

IHC only document types

Defining FI document types for specific IHC postings is advised. One new document type can be created for the IHC end-of-day postings, which we have defined as document type I1. It is also recommended to define another document type for IHC bank statement postings.

The IHC end-of-day process configuration consists of the following steps:

- ▶ Maintain GL Variant.
- ▶ Maintain GL Transaction.
- ▶ Assign transaction type to GL Transaction.
- ▶ Maintain GL Group.

▶ Define GL account assignment to current accounts.

▶ Transfer postings receivables/payables.

▶ Specify sequence of end-of-day processing chain.

Maintain GL Variant

GL Variants are defined to drive the postings of an in-house bank. The GL Variants are assigned at the bank area level (see the configuration step in Figure 8.1). For implementations with multiple bank areas that will have different postings, multiple GL Variants are defined. The GL Variant drives the process for posting the IHB activity to the SAP general ledger during the end-of-day process. All subsequent IHC end-of-day posting configuration is done by GL Variant.

The information specified with the GL Variant definition is: the chart of accounts, the IHC Detail Clearing account, and the document type used for posting the IHC activity to the SAP general ledger. Document type I1 – IHC EOD Postings – is used exclusively for the IHC end-of-day postings.

To define a GL Variant, follow the configuration menu path: FINANCIAL SUPPLY CHAIN MANAGEMENT • IN-HOUSE CASH • PERIODIC TASKS • GENERAL LEDGER TRANSFER • MAINTAIN GL VARIANTS (see Figure 8.39).

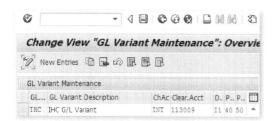

Figure 8.39: Definition of IHC GL Variant

Maintain GL Transaction

The GL Transactions are categories of IHC transactions. GL Transactions are the different types of IHC transaction categories that post differently and have different posting rules. In this step, the GL Transactions for the IHC transactions expected at an IHC are grouped by the GL

Variant that will be assigned to the bank area. Examples of IHC transactions are payments, debit interest, credit interest, taxes, fees, etc. In this step, the different GL Transactions are defined, as shown in Figure 8.40.

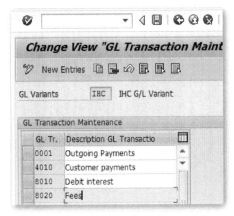

Figure 8.40: Definition of GL Transactions

Assign transaction type for payment transaction to GL Operation

Each IHC transaction expected at an IHC is assigned posting rules keys/GL Transactions, which drive how the IHC transactions post to the SAP general ledger. This step is done by GL Variant, which is assigned to the bank area (see Figure 8.41).

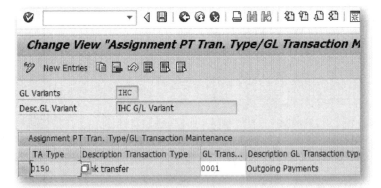

Figure 8.41: Assign payment item transaction type to GL transaction

Maintain GL Group

For the different types of IHC accounts (see Table 4.2), define GL Groups which drive the postings made for the different types of IHC accounts when they are posted to the SAP general ledger. Each IHC current account is assigned to a GL Group when the IHC current account is defined. The GL Groups are assigned to a GL Variant, which is assigned to a bank area. Note that unless the GL Group has been completely configured, it cannot be assigned in an IHC current account.

By defining GL Groups, the current accounts can be summarized into account groups (see Figure 8.42), which drives the postings for the activity sent through the current account.

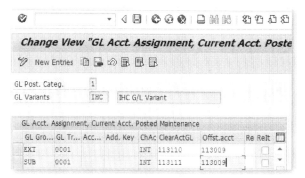

Figure 8.42: Definition of GL Groups

Define GL account assignment: current accounts

In this step, the G/L accounts to be used when the IHC current account activity is posted to the SAP general ledger are specified. You define which accounts are to be posted to first when the current account system items are transferred to the general ledger. The G/L accounts are specified by GL Group, GL Transaction, currency, and an additional key to be used in the case of customer-specific logic.

Enter the general ledger account to which the aggregated items are to be transferred (CLEARACTGL), and also an offsetting account - IHC EOD Technical Clearing account - for the corresponding general ledger posting, as shown in Figure 8.43. Note that all transactions related to a current account should be transferred to the same general ledger clearing account. Also, the G/L accounts entered here are clearing accounts that will be zero at the end of each day.

If the GL TRANSACTION is tax relevant, select the TAX ITEM (REIT) indicator and enter the appropriate FI tax key, determined by the sales tax rate.

As with the other IHC configuration, to make entering the configuration easier, default values can be specified by leaving the appropriate key fields blank.

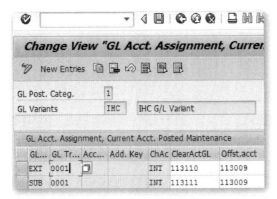

Figure 8.43: Define G/L accounts by GL group

Transfer postings payables/receivables

In this section, you define the receivables and payables G/L accounts to which the IHC account balances are transferred when the end-of-day process is run and the IHC activity is posted to the SAP general ledger. The GLACCTS RECS and GLACCTS PAYS accounts are the G/L accounts where the IHC current account balances remain after the end-of-day process is complete.

The balance of an IHC current account is first transferred to a clearing account (clearing account general ledger), and is then transferred to the appropriate receivables/payables account, depending on its +/- sign (see Figure 8.44).

Figure 8.44: Define posting payables/receivables G/L accounts

Include customer reports for mass processing

Instead of running the end-of-day processing steps manually each day, or creating scheduled jobs individually through the Define Background Job program (transaction code SM36), it is more efficient to have the end-of-day processing steps run as a daily scheduled job. To do this, a CHAIN ID is created in two configuration steps.

In the first step, the programs to be included in the end-of-day mass process chain are defined. In addition to the SAP standard end-of-day mass process programs, any customer-specific programs that need to be run as part of the IHC end-of-day process can also be entered here. To enter the programs, follow the configuration menu path: FINANCIAL SUPPLY CHAIN MANAGEMENT • IN-HOUSE CASH • PERIODIC TASKS • INCLUDE CUSTOMER REPORTS FOR MASS PROCESSING, as shown in Figure 8.45.

S...	Report Name	Description	Standard Variant	Job name
1	RFBKPDT2	Set Payment Transaction...	PROD	INCREMENT POSTING DATE
2	RFBKCONC	Account Balancing	PROD	ACCOUNT BALANCING
3	RFBKGLBSPREP	Balance Sheet Preparation	PROD	BALANCE SHEET PREP
4	RFBKGL01	General Ledger Transfer	PROD	FI TRANSFER
5	RFBKBSST	Bank Statement	PROD	SEND BANK STATEMENTS

Figure 8.45: Define programs in EOD processing chainSpecify sequence of mass processing

The next step is to define the order in which the programs assigned to the end-of-day mass processing are to be run. Only the programs that were assigned to be included in the end-of-day process chain can be assigned in this step. To enter the order of programs, follow the configuration menu path: FINANCIAL SUPPLY CHAIN MANAGEMENT • IN-HOUSE CASH • PERIODIC TASKS • SPECIFY SEQUENCE OF MASS PROCESSING and enter the programs (see Figure 8.46).

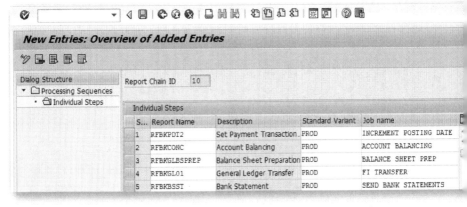

Figure 8.46: Define order of programs in end-of-day mass processing run

8.2   IHC house bank account definition

Any new bank accounts opened at external banks, that are to be used by the in-house bank, need to be created in SAP. As this step is not unique to IHC processing, the steps to create a house bank account have been omitted.

8.3   Treasury payment program

The IHC payments are executed in SAP using the Treasury payment program (transaction code F111). This payment program is very similar to the AP payment program (transaction code F110); but where the AP payment program pays AP and AR invoices, the Treasury payment program pays payment requests. For this reason, the Treasury payment program is also referred to as the Payment Program for Payment Requests. In this section, we will review the Treasury payment program and its configuration.

As with the AP payment program, there are three steps to running the Treasury payment program. The first step is to enter the parameters, which entails specifying which payment requests the user wants to pay. In the next step, the proposal run is executed. In the proposal run, SAP informs the user which payment requests, based on the parameters entered, are to be paid. In the third, and typically final step, both the accounting entries are made, and the payment medium is created. The payment medium is the payment file, such as an XML formatted file, that is transferred to the bank(s).

Like the AP payment program, the Treasury payment program can only be run for legal entities in the same country. (To determine the country of a legal entity, check the T001 table.) For global companies with a centralized Treasury department, this can be an issue, but usually not for IHC implementations.

8.3.1   Payment method/bank selection for payment program

The first step in configuring the Treasury payment program is to define the unique payment methods to be used. The payment methods used for this program should be different from those used for the AP payment program. One way to easily distinguish the payment methods for the Treasury payment program from those for the AP payment program is to use numbers 1-9 for the former and letters A-Z for the latter.

To get to the payment method configuration, follow the configuration menu path: FINANCIAL ACCOUNTING • ACCOUNTS RECEIVABLE AND ACCOUNTS PAYABLE • BUSINESS TRANSACTIONS • OUTGOING PAYMENTS • AUTOMATIC OUTGOING PAYMENTS • PAYMENT METHOD/BANK SELECTION FOR PAYMENT PROGRAM, or use transaction code FBZP.

The payment methods are defined at the country level and at the company code level. These steps are not shown here because they are the same steps that were completed for the AP payment methods. Please refer to Sections 7.3.1 and 7.3.2.

For our example scenario, the following payment methods are defined for the Treasury payment program:

▶ 1 – IHC Domestic Wire

▶ 2 – IHC Local payments (ACH/BACS/SEPA)

▶ 3 – IHC Cross Border Wire

In the country-specific settings, the selection shown in Figure 8.47 could be used for a low-value European payment.

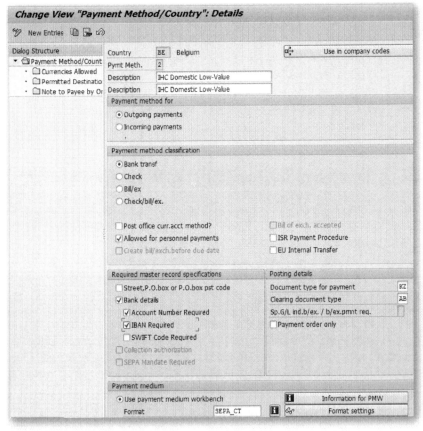

Figure 8.47: Definition of Treasury payment method

In the company-code-specific settings, select the FOREIGN BUSINESS PARTNER ALLOWED, FOREIGN CURRENCY ALLOWED, and CUST/VENDOR BANK ABROAD ALLOWED? indicators, assuming these types of payments are included in the project scope.

8.3.2   Define clearing account for payment requests

The next step is to assign the G/L account that will be the payment request clearing account, which will be used to track the IHC payment requests. The IHC payment requests are the IHC payments that will be sent to the external banks. These are the subsidiary's payments made on behalf of the IHC bank. This payment request clearing account was first mentioned in Chapter 4 of this book. To assign the G/L account, follow the configuration path: FINANCIAL SUPPLY CHAIN MANAGEMENT • TREASURY AND RISK MANAGEMENT • TRANSACTION MANAGER • GENERAL SETTINGS • PAYMENT MANAGEMENT • PAYMENT REQUESTS • DEFINE CLEARING ACCOUNT FOR PAYMENT REQUESTS (see Figure 8.48).

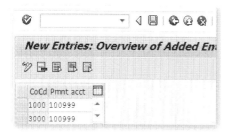

Figure 8.48: Define payment request clearing account

8.3.3   Define number ranges for payment requests

Next, define a number range for payment requests. Payment request numbers, also known as key numbers, go across company codes; this means that each payment request is given a unique number regardless of the company code the payment was made from. To define the payment request number range, follow the configuration path: FINANCIAL ACCOUNTING • BANK ACCOUNTING • BUSINESS TRANSACTIONS • PAYMENT TRANSACTIONS • PAYMENT REQUEST • DEFINE NUMBER RANGES FOR PAYMENT REQUESTS. Enter a number range 1 to 999999999, as shown in Figure 8.49.

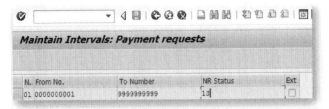

Figure 8.49: Define payment request number range

8.3.4 Check payment block reason

Next, create a payment block for Treasury payment requests. This blocks the Treasury payments from being paid by the AP payment program. We use payment block P for the Treasury payment request block. The payment blocking indicator must have the following properties: it cannot be changed in the payment proposal, it blocks manual payments, and it cannot be changed. Follow the configuration menu path: FINANCIAL ACCOUNTING • ACCOUNTS RECEIVABLE AND ACCOUNTS PAYABLE • BUSINESS TRANSACTIONS • OUTGOING PAYMENTS • MANUAL OUTGOING PAYMENTS • CHECK PAYMENT BLOCK REASON and define payment block P, as shown in Figure 8.50.

Block ind.	Description	Change in pmnt prop.	Manual payments block	Not changeable
	Free for payment	☑	☐	☐
*	Skip account	☐	☐	☐
A	Blocked for payment	☑	☑	☐
B	Blocked for payment	☑	☐	☐
N	IP postprocessing	☐	☐	☐
P	Payment request	☐	☑	☑

Figure 8.50: Define payment block properties

8.3.5 Define payment blocking indicators for accounting documents

The payment block is then assigned for Treasury payment requests by following the configuration menu path: FINANCIAL ACCOUNTING • BANK ACCOUNTING • BUSINESS TRANSACTIONS • PAYMENT TRANSACTIONS • PAYMENT REQUEST • DEFINE PAYMENT BLOCKING INDICATORS FOR ACCOUNTING DOCUMENTS (see Figure 8.51).

Figure 8.51: Assign payment block to payment requests

8.3.6 Define global settings

Follow the configuration path: FINANCIAL ACCOUNTING • BANK ACCOUNTING • BUSINESS TRANSACTIONS • PAYMENT TRANSACTIONS • PAYMENT HANDLING • DEFINE GLOBAL SETTINGS, to enter the Define Global Settings configuration. In this step, the account types required for the Treasury payment program, as selection fields, are specified. The account types are: origin of payment, customers, vendors, and G/L accounts. In the case of IHC payments, only select the ORIGIN field, although there is no harm in selecting the other account types. By selecting ORIGIN, the payment program can select payment requests to pay based on the origin of payment. In other words, users can pay by origin of the payment.

To keep the screen less busy and allow minimal options, select just the ORIGIN indicator, as shown in Figure 8.52.

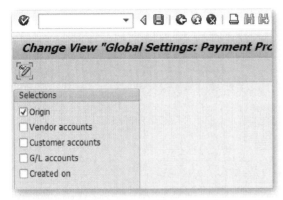

Figure 8.52: Global settings for payment requests

8.3.7 Enter origin indicators

The origin represents how the payment request was triggered and indicates the application area the payments originate from (i.e. CM, Treasury management, loans, etc.). In the case of IHC payments, the origin will be TR-IHC.

This configuration sets up:

▶ whether the payment program should check available amounts.

▶ which configuration should be used to drive the account determination for the Treasury payment program.

▶ whether existing attributes of an origin should be used to group payment requests with different origins.

▶ no posting of exchange rate differences.

Follow the configuration path: FINANCIAL ACCOUNTING • BANK ACCOUNTING • BUSINESS TRANSACTIONS • PAYMENT TRANSACTIONS • PAYMENT HANDLING • ENTER ORIGIN INDICATORS to specify the origin settings for the TR-IHC origin (see Figure 8.53).

Change View "Origin settings": Overview

New Entries

Origin settings

Origin	Name	Available amts	Account determ.	Grouping	No exchange ra...
TR-CM-BT	Bank Account Transfers	✓			
TR-IHC	In-House Cash	✓			
TR-LO	Loans Management	✓	✓		
TR-TM	Treasury Management	✓			

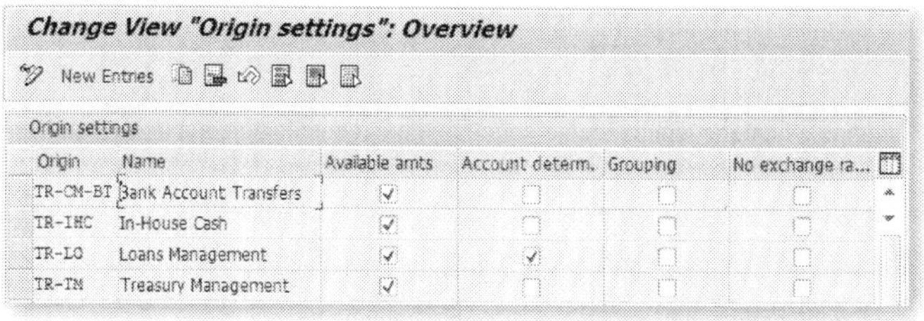

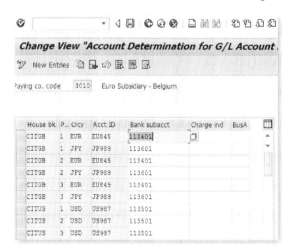

Figure 8.53: Define origin settings for the IHC payment origin

8.3.8 Define account determination

The account determination for the Treasury payment program needs to be entered. This configuration can be done by currency, house bank account, and/or payment method. In this step, you define when the Treasury payment program is run in the particular currency, from the particular house bank account, using the particular payment method; and the posting from the payment request clearing account should go to the cash clearing account specified here. In other words, when running the payment program this table is used to determine the accounting entries to be made. Follow the configuration menu path: FINANCIAL ACCOUNTING • BANK ACCOUNTING • BUSINESS TRANSACTIONS • PAYMENT TRANSACTIONS • PAYMENT HANDLING • BANK CLEARING ACCOUNT DETERMINATION • DEFINE ACCOUNT DETERMINATION and enter the configuration (see Figure 8.54).

Change View "Account Determination for G/L Account

New Entries

Paying co. code 3010 Euro Subsidiary - Belgium

House bk	P..	Crcy	Acct ID	Bank subacct	Charge ind	BusA
CITGB	1	EUR	EU845	113401		
CITGB	1	JPY	JP989	113601		
CITGB	2	EUR	EU845	113401		
CITGB	2	JPY	JP989	113601		
CITGB	3	EUR	EU845	113401		
CITGB	3	JPY	JP989	113601		
CITUS	1	USD	US987	113501		
CITUS	2	USD	US987	113501		
CITUS	3	USD	US987	113501		

Figure 8.54: Account determination for Treasury payment program

8.3.9   Define factory calendar per currency

You need to assign a factory calendar for each currency you use to pay out of the Treasury payment program. This is done using the configuration node: FINANCIAL ACCOUNTING • BANK ACCOUNTING • BUSINESS TRANSACTIONS • PAYMENT TRANSACTIONS • PAYMENT HANDLING • VALUE DATE • DEFINE FACTORY CALENDAR PER CURRENCY (see Figure 8.55).

Currency	Bank Co...	Region	Calendar ID	Text
AUD			AU	Factory calendar Australia standard
CAD			CA	Factory calendar Canada standard
CHF			CH	Factory calendar Switzerland standard
EUR			EU	European Monetary Union
GBP			GB	Factory calendar Great Britain standard
JPY			JP	Factory calendar Japan standard
NZD			AU	Factory calendar Australia standard
USD			US	Factory calendar US standard

Figure 8.55: Default calendar assignment by currency

8.4   Electronic bank statement processing

The electronic bank statement (EBS) configuration needs to be configured for both the IHC bank statements sent to the subsidiaries and for the bank statements from the external bank(s) for the external bank accounts used by the IHB. The EBS configuration steps required are the same whether the bank statement is an internally generated bank statement (e.g. one created by IHC), or an external bank statement. These steps were previously defined in Section 7.4, from an IHC bank statement perspective; therefore, we will not cover the configuration steps again here.

8.5 ALE configuration

SAP's IHC module uses ALE Intermediate Documents (IDocs) to pass information between the subsidiaries and the in-house bank. In this section, we cover the required ALE settings, which can be tricky. The information presented in this chapter assumes the subsidiaries and the in-house bank are in the same SAP client. If this is not the case, the ALE settings are slightly different.

ALE and IDoc processing

When implementing IHC, it is very helpful to have a good understanding of ALE and IDoc processing because this is how information is passed between the in-house bank participants and the in-house bank.

IDocs have a predetermined structure, and are used for passing information between SAP systems. The different types of IDocs pass information on different types of data. The two IDoc types relevant to IHC are the PAYEXT IDoc, which passes payment related data, and the FINSTA IDoc, which passes bank statement data. Each IDoc consists of a header, data segments and status records. Use transaction code WEDI to access the SAP EASY ACCESS IDoc AND EDI BASIS, which contains relevant information when working with ALE and IDocs (see Figure 8.56).

Accessing transaction code WEDI

WEDI is an area menu. To access WEDI, you must enter /oWEDI in the SAP command field located in the top left corner of the SAP window, or go to the SAP root screen.

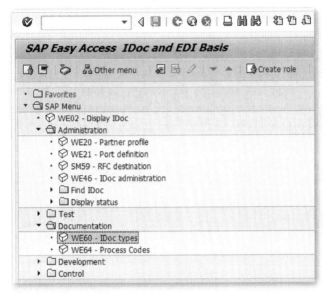

Figure 8.56: IDoc and EDI area menu

The ALE settings for our example scenario serve the following two purposes:

1. The information sent from the subsidiaries to the IHB are the payments, which are either payments to be made by the IHB on behalf of the subsidiary, or centralized incoming payments, which are to be executed by the IHB on behalf of the subsidiary. The payments are sent as PAYEXT (PEXR2002) IDocs. In addition, the bank statements sent from the IHB to the subsidiaries are FINSTA (FINSTA02) IDocs.

2. When IHC payment orders are transferred from the IHC subledger to a payment request during creation of an external payment, an outbound payment IDoc is sent by the IHB, and an inbound payment IDoc is received by the IHB.

To configure ALE for the above two purposes, the following steps are needed:

- ▶ Define the logical system.
- ▶ Define the target system for RFC calls.
- ▶ Create ports.
- ▶ Create partner profiles.

If multiple SAP systems are involved, an ALE distribution module is needed to define the messages passed between the SAP systems. The example in this book assumes the subsidiaries and IHB are in the same SAP instance, therefore, we will not look at creating an ALE distribution model.

For payment orders from companies affiliated with the in-house bank, or for cross-bank-area payment orders, use message type PAYEXT with basic type PEXR2002, and process code PEXN as the inbound parameter. For bank statements from the in-house bank to affiliated companies, use message type FINSTA with basic type FINSTA01, and the process code FINS as the inbound parameter.

For the payment order from the in-house bank to the clearing partner or executing system, use message type PAYEXT with basic type PEXR2002, and the process code PEXC as the inbound parameter. In this case, a payment request will be created.

Manual configuration

The RFC destinations, ports and partner profiles are not transportable and, therefore, need to be defined in each system.

8.5.1 Define logical system

For IHC purposes, logical systems correspond to a client. A logical system for the in-house bank and the subsidiaries' systems are needed.

To define a logical system, use transaction code SALE to get to the IDOC INTERFACE / APPLICATION LINK ENABLING (ALE) menu. Then select BASIC SETTINGS • LOGICAL SYSTEMS • DEFINE LOGICAL SYSTEM (see Figure 8.57).

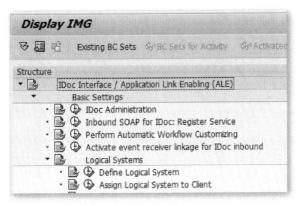

Figure 8.57: Creating logical systems

Define a logical system for your client, as shown in Figure 8.58.

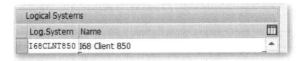

Figure 8.58: Creating logical systems for the IHC center

8.5.2 Assign logical system to client

Next, assign the logical system you created for the IHC center using this node by selecting the ASSIGN LOGICAL SYSTEM TO CLIENT option from the transaction code SALE, as previously shown in Figure 8.57. This step is shown in Figure 8.59.

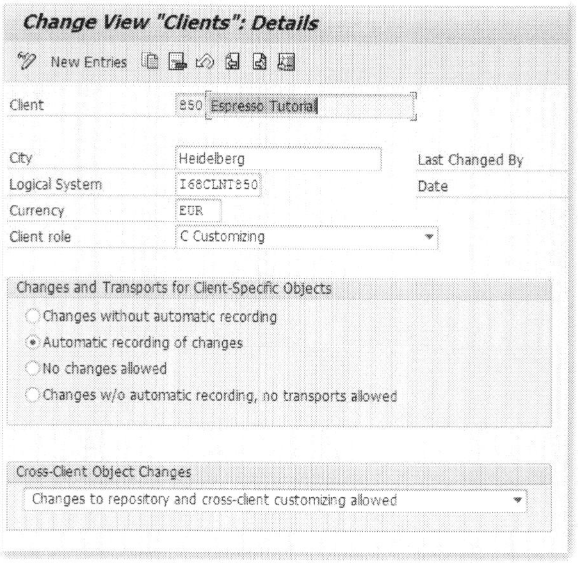

Figure 8.59: Assign logical system to client

8.5.3 Create RFC connections

Next, define the technical parameters for the RFC destinations using CREATE RFC CONNECTIONS by following the configuration menu path: SAP PORTFOLIO AND PROJECT MANAGEMENT • PORTFOLIO MANAGEMENT • BASE SYSTEM INTERFACES • SAP FINANCIAL AND CONTROLLING INTEGRATION • COMMON SYSTEM CONFIGURATION AND SAP FI-CO ALE SETUP • APPLICATION LINK ENABLING (ALE) • COMMUNICATION • CREATE RFC CONNECTIONS, or by entering transaction code SM59. This is required because the technical communication between the SAP systems is done by transactional Remote Function Calls (tRFC).

The Remote Function Call (RFC) is controlled by the RFC destination parameters. The name of the RFC destination can be the same as the logical system name created above. The Type of Entry must be type 3 (Connection to ABAP System), as shown in Figure 8.60.

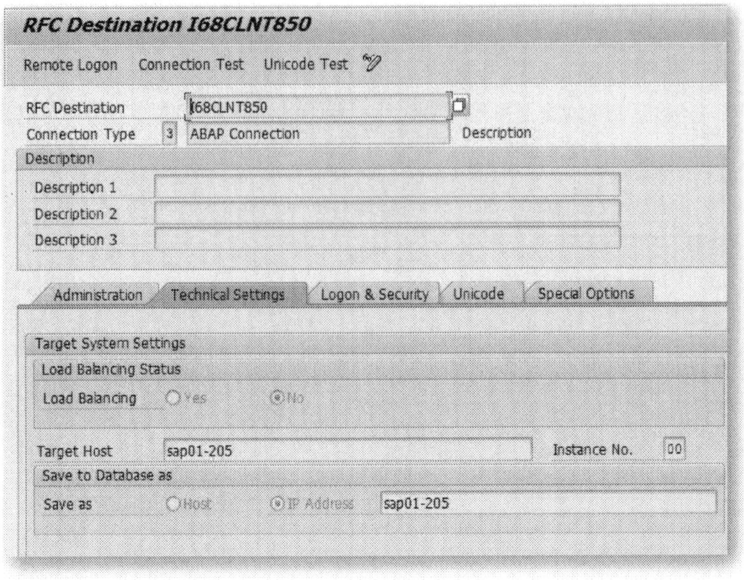

Figure 8.60: Create RFC connections

When creating an RFC destination, under the LOGON & SECURITY tab, you must assign specific logon credentials, or always have it use the current logged-on user's credentials (not shown).

8.5.4 Create ports

The next step is to create two ports, which can be completed by following the menu path: TOOLS • ALE • ALE ADMINISTRATION • RUNTIME SETTINGS • PORT MAINTENANCE, or by executing transaction code WE21. The first port is a transactional RFC port, which is needed if the in-house bank and the subsidiary companies are in the same system, as in our example. For a description, enter IHC_PORT (see Figure 8.61).

In addition, create a file port for the EUPEXR IDocs that are not needed for the IHC processing, but that will be created by SAP with the PAYEXT IDocs. When a PAYEXT IDoc is created, a corresponding EUPEXR IDoc is created automatically by SAP. The EUPEXR IDoc is not needed, so we create a file port called NONE (see Figure 8.62), which will be set as the port for the EUPEXR IDoc. (For more information, see SAP note

527431.) The files generated in this port can be deleted at specific intervals.

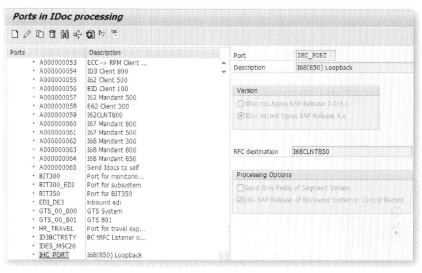

Figure 8.61: Create transactional RFC IHC_PORT

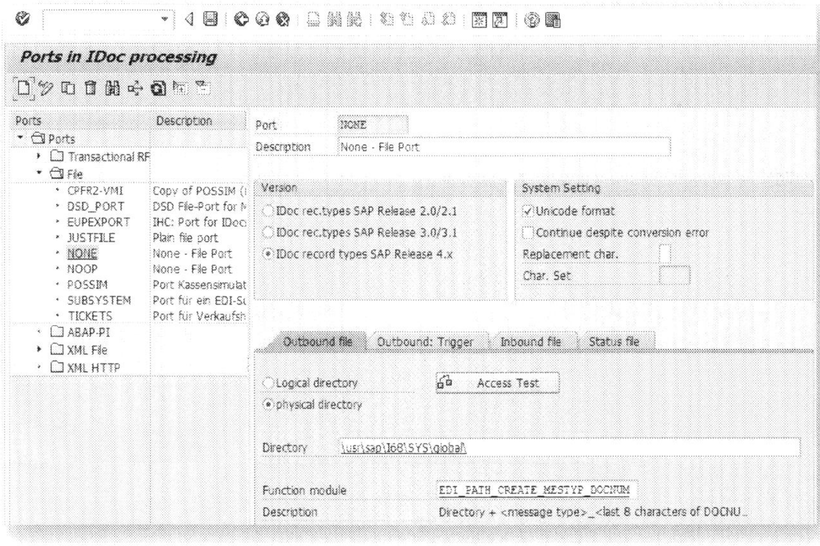

Figure 8.62: Create port NONE

8.5.5 Create partner profiles

Partner profiles are needed for data exchange when using ALE, as is the case with the IHC module. Three types of partner profiles are needed: bank, logical system and business partner. Partner profiles are created by following the menu path: TOOLS • ALE • ALE ADMINISTRATION • RUNTIME SETTINGS • PARTNER PROFILES, or by executing transaction code WE20.

For the first type of partner profile, for each IHC center, create a 'Bank' partner profile. The 'Bank' partner profile will send PAYEXT IDocs and receive bank statement FINSTA IDocs when passing information between the subsidiaries and the in-house bank. Figure 8.63 shows how to create it.

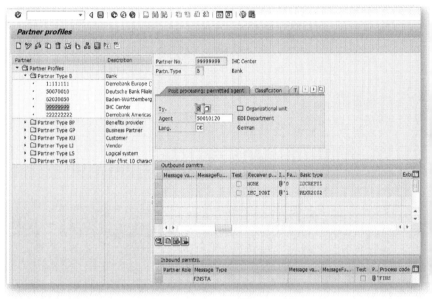

Figure 8.63: Define the IHC 'Bank' partner profile

You need to define two logical system partner profiles for ALE communication, as well as the required inbound and outbound parameters. The LOCAL and I68CLNT850 partner profiles should have mirror image IDoc settings based on our example scenario. This is because the LOCAL partner profile sends out the payment IDocs when creating a payment request, and the I68CLNT850 partner profile receives and processes the payment IDocs.

The LOCAL partner profile settings are displayed in Figure 8.64.

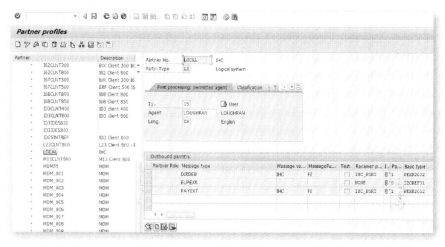

Figure 8.64: Definition of the LOCAL partner profile

The I68CLNT850 partner profile settings are displayed in Figure 8.65.

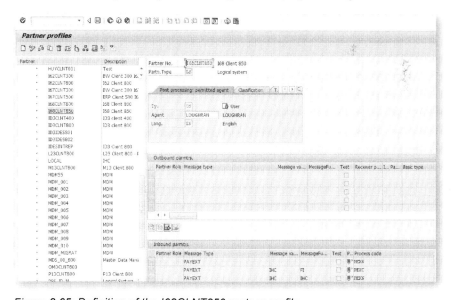

Figure 8.65: Definition of the I68CLNT850 partner profile

In addition, a Business Partner (partner type GP, not BP – this is not a typo) partner profile should be created for each subsidiary that will have an account at the IHB. Before creating the business partner profiles, the business partners need to be created in the client. Figure 8.66 shows a business partner profile for SUB_2100. Note the OUTBOUND PARMTRS. and INBOUND PARMTRS. boxes where the outbound and inbound IDoc message types are entered. Use the 🖼 icon and copy icon 🖻 to add new message types.

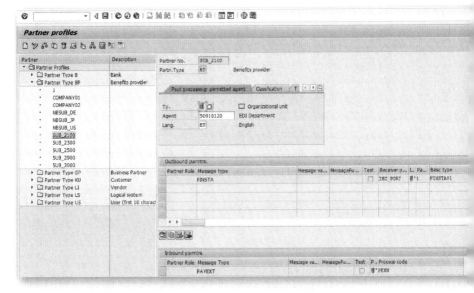

Figure 8.66: Partner profile creation – Business Partner

The detail for the outgoing (bank statement) FINSTA IDocs is shown in Figure 8.67.

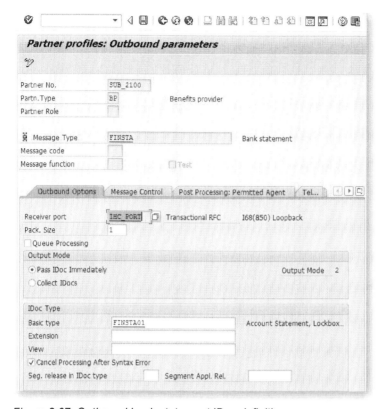

Figure 8.67: Outbound bank statement IDoc definition

The detail for the incoming (payment) PAYEXT IDoc is shown in Figure 8.68. The process code PEXN indicates that a payment order should be created when this payment IDoc is processed.

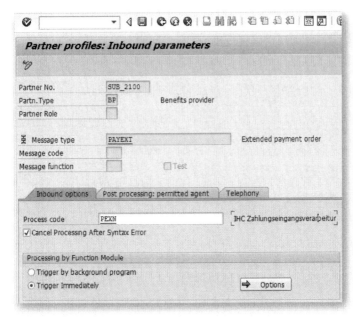

Figure 8.68: Inbound payment PAYEXT IDoc definition

After creating one business partner profile, use the copy icon to create subsequent profiles.

9 Resolving configuration issues

In this chapter, we provide pointers for resolving common issues encountered after configuring the IHC module.

We suggest that after doing the configuration, the functionality in logical sections be tested. For example, after completing the IHC configuration, first test a manual internal payment order; internal payment orders require less configuration than external payment orders. After that, test the configuration of the Treasury payment program by entering a free-form payment or a repetitive code payment. Once you have confirmed that all the configuration is complete, test entering an external payment order.

9.1 Errors when posting payment orders

The screenshot in Figure 9.1 shows a payment order that errored when it was posted. Note that the indicator in the ERROR column is selected for the second payment order.

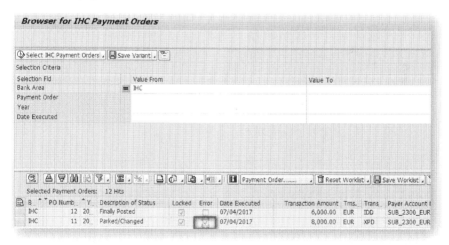

Figure 9.1: Errored payment order

By double-clicking on the payment order, we can drill down to see the details of it, as shown in Figure 9.2. In this case, it is an external payment order from the SUB_2300_EUR account.

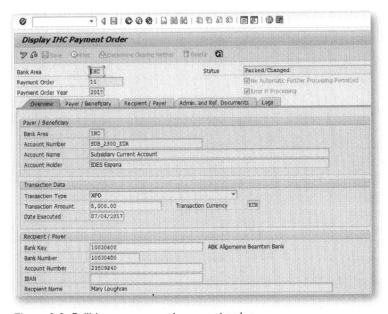

Figure 9.2: Drilldown on errored payment order

By selecting the LOGS tab, we can see that the payment order has not been posted successfully, as shown in Figure 9.3.

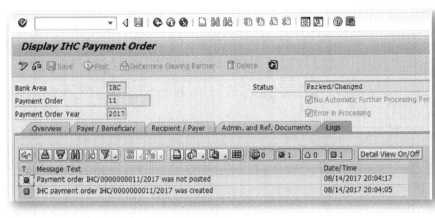

Figure 9.3: Errored payment order LOGS tab

By selecting the DETAIL VIEW ON/OFF button, SAP shows us its detailed processing, indicating exactly where the issue is (see Figure 9.4).

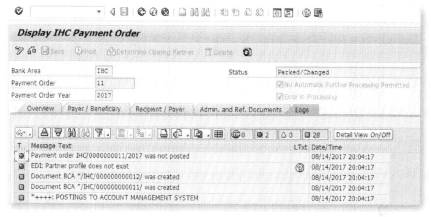

Figure 9.4: Expanded detail log

With the additional information provided in the detailed log, we see that the error is due to a missing EDI partner profile. We then create the missing EDI partner profile, which in this case is the highlighted row in Figure 9.5.

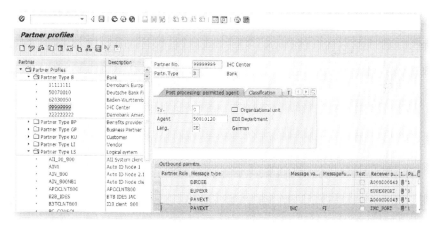

Figure 9.5: Missing partner profile for external payment creation

We then re-post the payment order through IHC0 by selecting the row of the payment order, right-clicking to get to the menu shown in Figure 9.6, and then selecting POST from the menu. The payment order is now successfully posted to the IHC subledger.

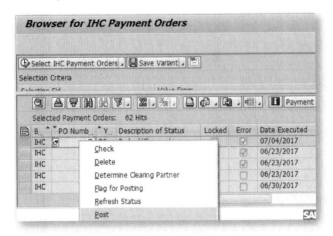

Figure 9.6: Browser for IHC payment orders popup menu

If you receive the error shown in Figure 9.7 and Figure 9.8 on the incoming PAYEXT IDoc into the in-house bank, it means that SAP is not able to determine a transaction type for the payment order it is attempting to create. Check the configuration settings in the configuration node: FINANCIAL SUPPLY CHAIN MANAGEMENT • IN-HOUSE CASH • ACCOUNT MANAGEMENT • PAYMENT PROCESSES IN IN-HOUSE CASH • DEFINE TRANSACTION TYPE FOR AUTOMATIC PAYMENTS, or look in table IHC_TAB_APM_TT. It is in these configuration settings that SAP determines a payment order transaction type based on the in-house bank, the AP payment method, the currency of the payment, and the recipient's bank country.

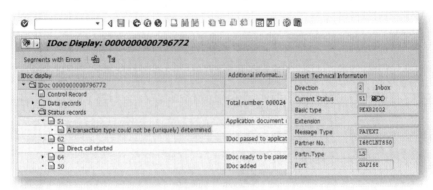

Figure 9.7: Inbound PAYEXT IDoc error to the IHB

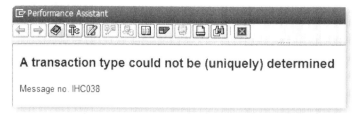

Figure 9.8: Detailed error message

9.2 Errors when creating an external payment

If you receive the error shown in Figure 9.9 and Figure 9.10 on the in-coming PAYEXT IDoc into the in-house bank, check the configuration settings in the configuration node: FINANCIAL SUPPLY CHAIN MANAGEMENT • IN-HOUSE CASH • ACCOUNT MANAGEMENT • PAYMENT PROCESSES IN IN-HOUSE CASH • OUTGOING PAYMENT ORDER • SET UP CREATION OF PAYMENT REQUESTS FOR INBOUND IDOCS IN FI, or look in table IHC_DB_INB _ACCTS. It is in these configuration settings that SAP determines the clearing partner for the payment.

Figure 9.9: Error on an incoming PAYEXT IDoc to the IHB

Figure 9.10: Error message on an incoming PAYEXT IDoc to the IHB

If you receive the error NO PAYMENT METHOD ENTERED: MESSAGE NO. PZ014 (see Figure 9.11 and Figure 9.12) on the incoming PAYEXT IDoc into the in-house bank when creating a payment request from a payment order, first check the payment method in the outgoing PAYEXT IDoc from the in-house bank to ensure the expected payment method was determined: FINANCIAL SUPPLY CHAIN MANAGEMENT • IN-HOUSE CASH • ACCOUNT MANAGEMENT • PAYMENT PROCESSES IN IN-HOUSE CASH • MAKE BASIC SETTINGS FOR PAYMENT PROCESSES • PAYMENT METHOD DATA configuration. The payment method to check is in the E1IDKU3-PAIRZAWE IDoc segment, as shown in Figure 9.13. This payment method should be a Treasury payment program (transaction code F111) payment method and not an AP payment method. If it is an AP payment method, the above configuration is incorrect because SAP is unable to determine a payment method for the payment request it is trying to create.

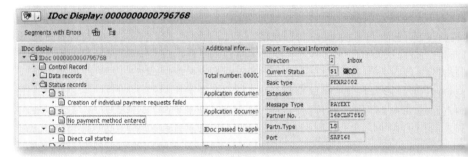

Figure 9.11: Inbound PAYEXT IDoc to create payment request

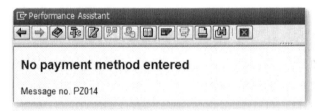

Figure 9.12: Detailed error message

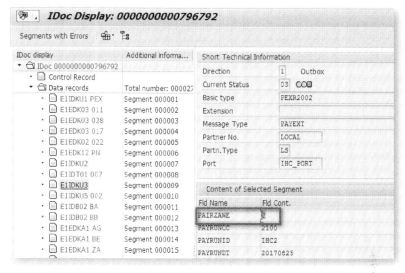

Figure 9.13: Payment method field in PAYEXT IDoc

Assuming the payment method in the outbound PAYEXT IDoc from the in-house bank is correct, check the configuration settings in the configuration node: FINANCIAL SUPPLY CHAIN MANAGEMENT • IN-HOUSE CASH • ACCOUNT MANAGEMENT • PAYMENT PROCESSES IN IN-HOUSE CASH • OUTGOING PAYMENT ORDER • SET UP CREATION OF PAYMENT REQUESTS FOR INBOUND IDOCS IN FI in the ACCOUNT DETAILS folder, or look in table IHC_DB_INB_ACCTS.

9.3 Errors in the IHC end-of-day process

If errors are encountered when running the IHC end-of-day process, they are displayed in the corresponding APPLICATION LOGS programs found by following the menu path: ACCOUNTING • FINANCIAL SUPPLY CHAIN MANAGEMENT • IN-HOUSE CASH • PERIODIC PROCESSING • APPLICATION LOGS (see Figure 9.14).

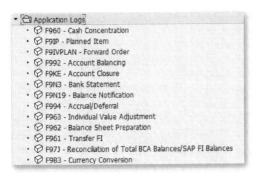

Figure 9.14: IHC end-of-day APPLICATION LOGS

If the error message shown in Figure 9.15 is displayed after running the Mass Run for internal bank statements program (transaction code F9N1), go to the Bank Statement Application Logs program (transaction code F9N3), to view the errors encountered.

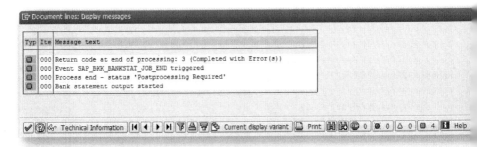

Figure 9.15: Unsuccessful mass run of IHC bank statements

Figure 9.16 shows the input screen to the IHC bank statement application log program. When it is executed, the date and time fields automatically populate to the current date and time. The user only needs to execute the program.

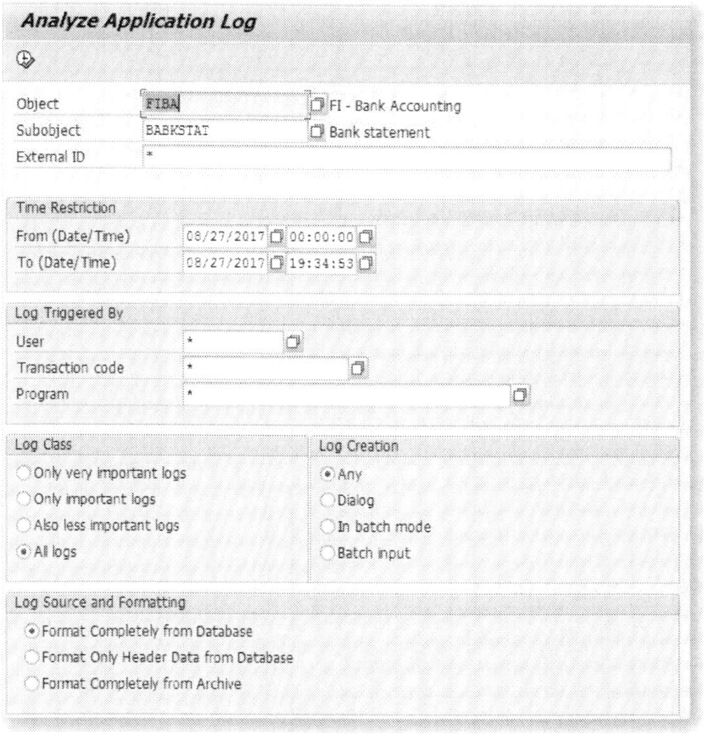

Figure 9.16: IHC bank statement application log input screen

Figure 9.17 shows the output screen of the IHC bank statement application log program. The data is displayed with the most recent run at the bottom. The traffic lights help the user to find runs that have errored (red traffic light), or that have warnings (yellow traffic light). Double-clicking on an error or a warning displays details of the issue in the MESSAGE TEXT window.

235

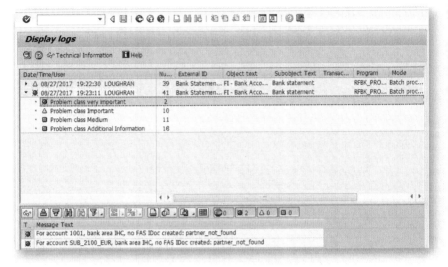

Figure 9.17: IHC bank statement application log output screen

To resolve the issue, first check the settings in the current account SUB_2100_EUR on the ACCOUNT STATEMENTS tab, as shown in Figure 9.18. The PARTNER the FINSTA bank statements are sent to for this current account is SUB_2100; therefore, there must be a partner profile of Partner Type GP (Business Partner) defined for SUB_2100, and the partner profile must have the message type FINSTA defined as an outgoing IDoc. This should be validated.

The current account's ACCOUNT STATEMENT settings look good. Looking at the APPLICATION LOG a second time, we can see that there is a warning message, as shown at the bottom of the screen in Figure 9.19.

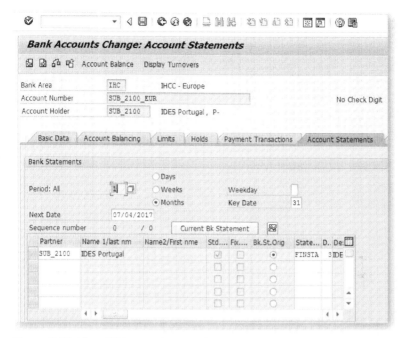

Figure 9.18: View IHC current account

Figure 9.19: Warning message in bank statement application log

After pressing the long text icon, we see the full warning message, as shown in Figure 9.20.

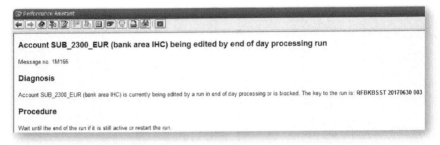

Figure 9.20: Detailed IHC bank statement error

To resolve this issue, the SAP function module BKK_PA_PROCESS_ DESTRUCTOR must be run to unlock the processes that are locked. The necessary steps are outlined below.

First, run the Function Builder program by following the menu path: TOOLS • ABAP WORKBENCH • DEVELOPMENT • FUNCTION BUILDER, or by executing transaction code SE37. Enter the text BKK_PA_PROCESS_ DESTRUCTOR in the Function Module field, as shown in Figure 9.21.

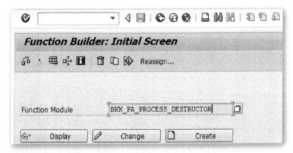

Figure 9.21: Execute function module BKK_PA_PROCESS_DESTRUCTOR

Press the test/execute icon ▦, then double-click on the row shown in Figure 9.22.

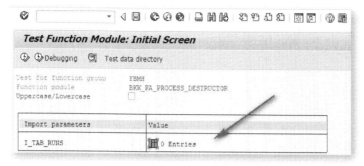

Figure 9.22: Enter import parameters

Enter the information from the error displayed in Figure 9.20 (see Figure 9.23).

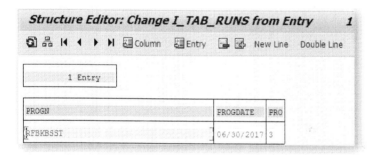

Figure 9.23: Error parameters entered

Green arrow back once, press the execute icon, and the screen shown in Figure 9.24 is displayed.

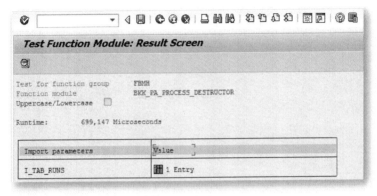

Figure 9.24: Function module executed

At this point, the Start Bank Statement program (transaction code F9N1) should be re-run, as shown in Figure 9.25.

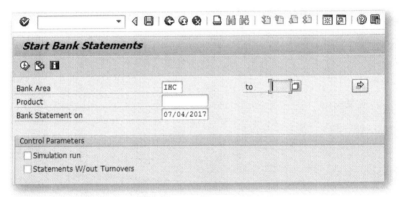

Figure 9.25: Restart the mass bank statement run

After the Start Bank Statement program (transaction code F9N1) is re-run, the message in Figure 9.26 is displayed.

Note: the Start Bank Statements - Restart program can be found by following the menu path: ACCOUNTING • FINANCIAL SUPPLY CHAIN MANAGEMENT • IN-HOUSE CASH • PERIODIC PROCESSING • BANK STATEMENT • RESTART, or by executing transaction code F9N4. It can be executed to restart the bank statement run program that previously had errors.

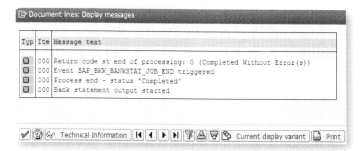

Figure 9.26: Successful run of the mass bank statements

9.4 Errors with centralized incoming payments

The centralized incoming payments scenario is initiated when importing a bank statement that has specific text in the note to payee field to trigger the creation of a payment order. When importing the bank statement, if the error message shown in Figure 9.27 is displayed, then SAP has recognized the specific text in the note to payee field, but the configuration in the Define Transaction Types for Incoming Payment should be adjusted. (The error message is TRANSACTION TYPE FOR ACTIVITY CATEGORY BAI2 AND BTC 195 WAS NOT DETERMINED.)

Figure 9.27: Bank statement import error with ROBO

When you encounter this error, check the configuration settings in the configuration node: FINANCIAL SUPPLY CHAIN MANAGEMENT • IN-HOUSE CASH • ACCOUNT MANAGEMENT • PAYMENT PROCESSES IN IN-HOUSE CASH • CENTRAL CASH RECEIPT / INCOMING BANK STATEMENTS • DEFINE TRANSACTION TYPES FOR INCOMING PAYMENT. Specifically check the EXTERNAL TRANSACTION field. If the EXTERNAL TRANSACTION field is left blank, the field becomes a wildcard, and any BTC would be accepted, as shown in Figure 9.28.

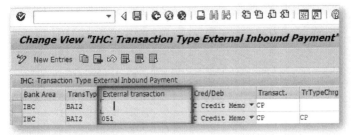

Figure 9.28: External transaction (BTC) for centralized payment

10 Tips, tricks and other useful information

In this chapter, we cover tips and tricks that are helpful in an SAP IHC implementation. We also give a list of definitions and of transaction codes relevant to IHC processing.

10.1.1 Tips and tricks

Reprocessing IDocs

Having experience working with IDocs is an advantage when implementing or supporting SAP's IHC module.

The Test Tool for IDoc Processing program (transaction code WE19) is very useful during an IHC implementation. This can be used to copy an errored IDoc and re-generate it after the issues that caused the error have been resolved. Below is an example of how WE19 can be used. In Figure 10.1, we see a successful outbound IDoc from the in-house bank to subsidiary 2100, but the inbound IDoc has failed. Note the red status on the inbound IDoc.

Figure 10.1: Errored inbound bank statement IDoc

Drilling down into the errored IDoc, we see a message saying that the corresponding Application Logs should be checked, as shown in Figure 10.2.

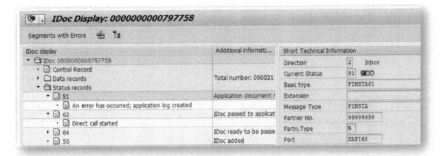

IDoc display	Additional informati...	Short Technical Information		
▼ 🗀 IDoc 0000000000797758		Direction	2	Inbox
• 🗀 Control Record		Current Status	51	✖OO
▶ 🗀 Data records	Total number: 000021	Basic type	FINSTA01	
▼ 🗀 Status records		Extension		
▼ 🗀 51	Application document r	Message Type	FINSTA	
• 🗀 An error has occurred; application log created		Partner No.	99999999	
▼ 🗀 62	IDoc passed to applicat	Partn.Type	B	
• 🗀 Direct call started		Port	SAPI68	
▶ 🗀 64	IDoc ready to be passe			
• 🗀 50	IDoc added			

Figure 10.2: Message in errored bank statement IDoc

The IHC Application Logs can be found by following the menu path: Accounting • Financial Supply Chain Management • In-House Cash •
Periodic Processing • Application Logs • Bank Statement. The input
screen defaults to the current time, as shown in Figure 10.3.

Analyze Application Log

Object	FIBA	FI - Bank Accounting
Subobject	BABKSTAT	Bank statement
External ID	*	

Time Restriction

From (Date/Time)	08/31/2017	00:00:00
To (Date/Time)	08/31/2017	03:14:45

Log Triggered By

User	*
Transaction code	*
Program	*

Log Class	Log Creation
○ Only very important logs	◉ Any
○ Only important logs	○ Dialog
○ Also less important logs	○ In batch mode
◉ All logs	○ Batch input

Figure 10.3: Bank statement application logs

Press the execute icon ⊕ to see the most recent errors, as shown in
Figure 10.4 The error here indicates that the partner profile is missing for

the business partner associated with the current account EXT_3010_ EUR, which is business partner SUB_3010.

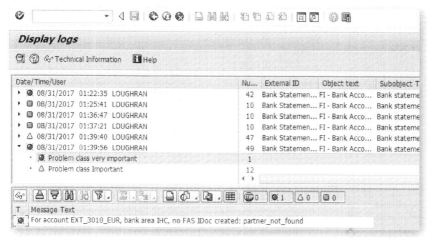

Figure 10.4: Bank statement application log error message

After resolving the issue, the fastest way to retest is to import the failed IDoc again. This is where WE19 comes in. We now go to transaction code WE19 and on the input screen enter the failed IDoc, as shown in Figure 10.5.

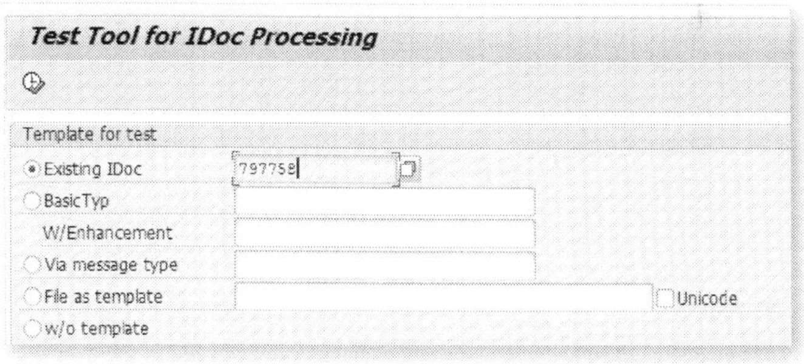

Figure 10.5: Reprocess IDoc 797758 using WE19

Press the execute icon ⊕, and a screen similar to the one in Figure 10.6 is displayed. It shows the body of the IDoc that was entered on the input screen. From here, you can make updates to any of the fields in the IDoc body, if necessary; for example, to test what effect certain changes would have on the processing of the IDoc. You then press the STANDARD

245

Inbound button to have SAP reprocess the IDoc. Note that the Standard Inbound button is pressed because we are re-importing an inbound IDoc. If we were going to re-process an outbound IDoc, the Standard Outbound Processing button would be pressed.

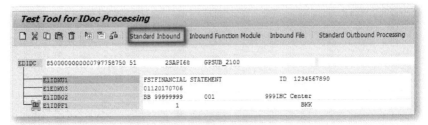

Figure 10.6: Start to reprocess an inbound IDoc

A popup like the one in Figure 10.7 is displayed. Press the Continue (Enter) icon ✅ to reprocess the IDoc. Note that the function module that processes the FINSTA IDoc is IDOC_INPUT_FINSTA, which can be seen in the screenshot in Figure 10.7.

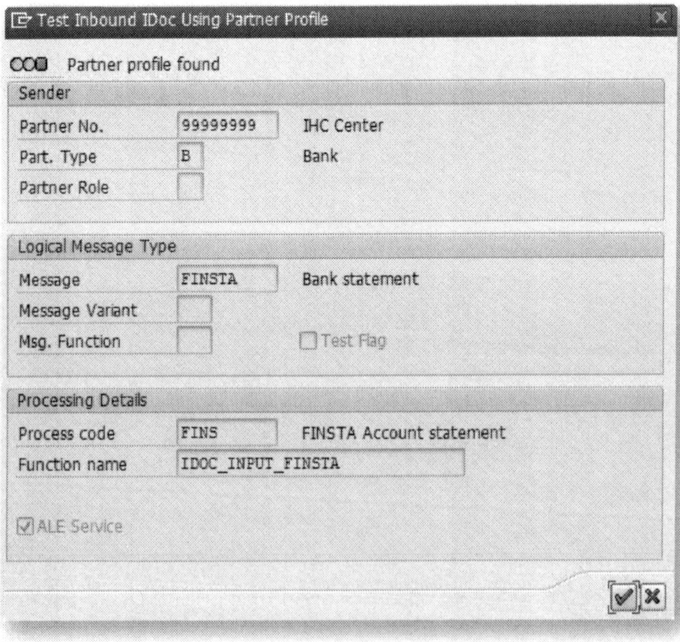

Figure 10.7: Reprocess inbound FINSTA IDoc from WE19

Reporting on a current account

By viewing the IHC virtual accounts, users can see all information (including payments and historical bank statements) relevant to the accounts. To view an IHC virtual account, follow the menu path: ACCOUNTING • FINANCIAL SUPPLY CHAIN MANAGEMENT • IN-HOUSE CASH • ACCOUNT • CHANGE, or execute transaction code F9K2. The input screen to this program is shown in Figure 10.8.

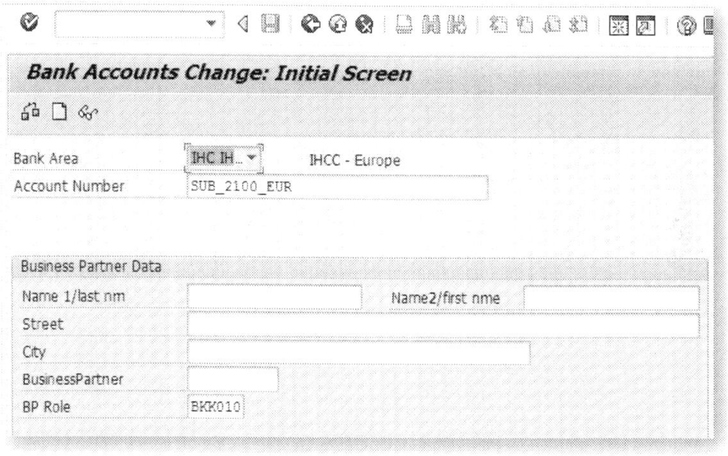

Figure 10.8: Change IHC current account

All relevant information relating to the IHC virtual accounts are stored in the IHC account master data, as displayed in Figure 10.9.

Users can select the ACCOUNT BALANCE button or DISPLAY TURNOVERS button to display the account balance or the payment transactions made through an IHC virtual account. Press the DISPLAY TURNOVERS button and enter the desired date range (see Figure 10.10). Press return.

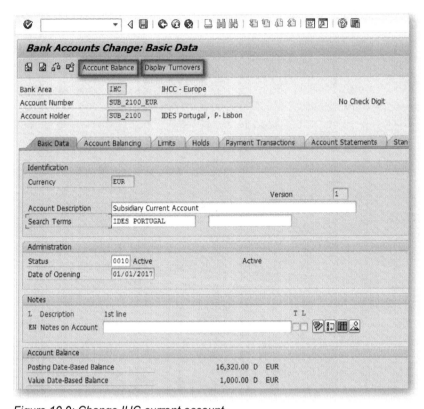

Figure 10.9: Change IHC current account

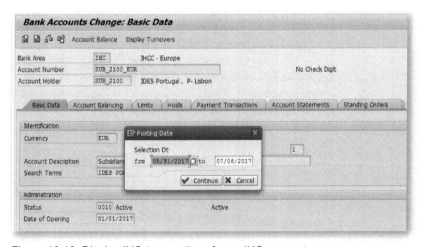

Figure 10.10: Display IHC transactions for an IHC account

The system displays the payment orders in reverse order (last payment order executed is shown first), as shown in Figure 10.11.

Bank Accounts Change: Basic Data

| ◀ ◀ ▶ ▶| 🔍 🖨 ▽ ▽ ⬚ ⅗ 🗗 🗗 Choose | | 🗊 🗊 Selections | NA Currency | TA Currency |

```
nover List                              08/31/2017                                    00:39:09 Time

k Area       IHC                       IHCC - Europe
ount Number                         SUB_2100_EUR
ount Holder IDES Portugal / P- Lisbon

ount  Balance  on  07/06/2017
ting Date                    16,320.00- EUR
ue Date                       1,000.00- EUR

ument  Overview        05/31/2017 - 07/06/2017

    Item number Item Post. date Value date Posting Text              CACur        Amount in AC
    Ref. Bank Key   Reference Account Number        Reference Name of Account Holder

         33    1 07/05/2017 08/29/2017 Bank transfer            EUR           9,000.00-
    10030600      67879889                     ICYOU PORTUGAL S.A.
         31    1 07/04/2017 08/25/2017 Bank transfer            EUR              99.00-
    10030600      67879889                     ICYOU PORTUGAL S.A.
         29    1 07/04/2017 08/25/2017 Bank transfer            EUR             666.00-
    10030600      67879889                     ICYOU PORTUGAL S.A.
```

Figure 10.11: History of IHC payment order for IHC account

From here, users can drill down to the payment order and payment items. It is also possible to change the display variant on this screen to view other payment-related fields.

When selecting the ACCOUNT STATEMENTS tab (refer back to Figure 10.9), you can navigate to either the current bank statement or historical bank statements. To see the current bank statement, which has not yet been sent, press the CURRENT BK STATEMENT button. To view the historical bank statements, press the Historical Bk Statements icon 🖾, as shown in Figure 10.12.

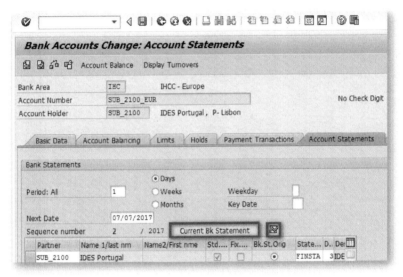

Figure 10.12: Viewing bank statements for IHC current account

Figure 10.13 shows the historical bank statements for the SUB_2100_EUR current account. To view the full bank statement contents of any of the historical bank statements, double-click on any of the lines displayed.

Bank Accounts Change: Account Statements

```
Bank Area:        IHC
Account number: SUB_2100_EUR
Account Currency: EUR
```

Bk.Stat.Yr	Bk.St. No.	Date	Time	PostngDate	Beginning Balance	End Balance	Crcy
2017	2	08/31/2017	01:39:54	07/06/2017	7,320.00-	16,320.00-	EUR
2017	1	08/28/2017	04:21:48	07/04/2017	0.00	7,320.00-	EUR

Figure 10.13: Viewing historical bank statements

10.1.2 Definition of terms

Table 10.1 contains definitions of key terms used in this book.

Term	Definition
ALE	Application Link Enabling. ALE is the technology the IHC module uses to structure data between the different organizational units included in the process.
bilateral netting	Bilateral netting is a process by which two parties (supplier and vendor) reduce or aggregate the overall number of transactions (payables and receivables) between them.
company code	An organizational term in SAP used to identify a legal entity or subsidiary of a corporate group. In this book, the terms subsidiary and company code are used interchangeably.
current account	A current account is a bank account at the In-House Cash bank. A current account and virtual account are the same thing. In this book, we use the terms current account and virtual account interchangeably.
IDoc	IDoc stands for Intermediate Document. IDocs define structured formats to pass specific information, such as payments and bank statement data, when using ALE.
IHB	In-House Bank. This term refers to the in-house bank. IHB and IHCC are used interchangeably in this book.
IHC	In-House Cash. When this term is used it refers specifically to SAP's IHC module.
multilateral netting	Multilateral netting is the management of payables and receivables resulting in a net receipt or payment to each entity in their local and/or preferred currency. The process can be managed centrally using an in-house bank or a shared service center.
participant	Legal entity or company code that has an account at the in-house bank.
partner profile	A partner profile specifies the various characteristics of data that is exchanged with a business partner. It also defines how the data is changed.
payment item	A payment order consists of at least two payment items. The payment items are the debit and credit sides of the payment order.
payment order	A payment order is a payment at/sent through the in-house bank.

251

Term	Definition
POBO	POBO stands for payments on behalf of.
ROBO	ROBO stands for receivables on behalf of, which is the same as centralized receipts.
reconciliation key	Reconciliation keys summarize the posting data that is posted from SAP subledgers where high volumes of transactions are anticipated, such as IHC to the SAP general ledger. This means the IHC activity does not post individually to the SAP general ledger. It posts in summarized postings.
subsidiary	Legal entity or company code that has an account at the in-house bank. In this book, the terms subsidiary and company code are used interchangeably.
virtual account	A virtual account is a bank account at the in-house cash bank. A virtual account and current account are the same thing. In this book, we use the terms current account and virtual account interchangeably.

Table 10.1: Definition of IHC terms

10.1.3 Transaction code listing

The following tables list the different transaction codes relating to SAP's IHC processing.

In addition, entering FSCM-IHC in the SAP command field takes the user to the SAP Easy Access menu for In-House Cash.

Table 10.2 contains IHC master data transaction codes.

Transaction code	Description
FIHC	Create In-House Cash Center
FI01	Create Bank
FI02	Change Bank
FI03	Display Bank
FI06	Set Flag to Delete Bank
BP	Maintain Business Partner

Transaction code	Description
FK02	Change Vendor
FD02	Change Customer
F9K1	Create Account
F9K2	Change Account
F9K3	Display Account
F9KAC	Release Account Closure
F9KD	Account Closure
F9KE	Application Log Account Closure
FIPRD3	Display Product
F983	Display General Conditions
F982	Edit General Conditions
F98E	Edit Condition Assignment
F98F	Display Condition Assignment

Table 10.2: Master data transaction codes

Table 10.3 contains IHC payment order-related transaction codes.

Transaction code	Description
F9I3	Display Payment Order
F9IG	Reverse Payment Item
F9I7	Display Payment Item
IHC0	Payment Order Browser
IHC1EP	Create External Payment Order (outgoing)
IHC1ED	Create External Payment Order - debit memo (incoming)
IHC1IP	Create Internal Payment Order (outgoing)
IHC1ID	Create Internal Payment Order – debit memo (incoming)
IHC2	Change Payment Order
IHC3	Display Payment Order

Table 10.3: IHC account management transaction codes

Table 10.4 contains end-of-day processing transaction codes.

Transaction code	Description
F9B1	Posting Cut-off Payment Transactions
F9KD	Account Closure
F9N7	Create Bank Statement - Single Account
F9N1	Create Bank Statements - Mass Run
F9N4	Restart - Bank Statement
F9HL	Balance Sheet Preparation BCA – GL
F9HI	Transfer BCA - GL
F9N11	Start End-of-Day Processing
F9N10	Overview End-of-Day Processing
F9N12	Overview of Current Mass Runs
F9N8	List of Accounts in End-of-Day Processing
F9KE	Application Log Account Closure
F9N3	Application Log Bank Statement
F962	Application Log Balance Sheet Prep.
F961	Application Log FI Transfer
F9J0	Display Application Log
F97J	Application log for Balance Sheet Preparation
F9B1	Posting Cut-off Payment Transactions
F9KD	Account Closure
F991	Mass Account Balancing
F996	Single Account Balancing (Int./Charge)
F995	Restart Account Balancing
F99F	Single Account Balancing: Restart
FF.6	Display Electronic Bank Statement

Table 10.4: End-of-day processing transaction codes

Table 10.5 contains IHC reporting transaction codes.

Transaction code	Description
F9HIST_KOND_INDIV	History of Individual Conditions
F9HIST_KOND_STAND	History of Standard Conditions
F9HIST_KOND_ZUORD	History of the Condition Assignment
F970_VAL	Balance List by Key Date
F970	Account Balances
F971	Account Locks
F9A8	Check Locks
F973	Display reconciliation balance list 1
F974	Display reconciliation balance list 2
F97I	Reconciliation - total BCA Balances with SAP FI Balances
F97E	Recon. to reconciliation key
F97G	Statement FI Document/BCA Posting (List of the BCA Postings for One FI Document Line)
F97A	Overview of the BCA Reconciliation Keys
F97A1	Reconciliation key detail display
F97AT	Audit Trail

Table 10.5: Reporting transaction codes

Table 10.6 contains miscellaneous transaction codes.

Transaction code	Description
WE02	Display IDoc
WE19	Test Tool for IDoc Processing
WE60	Documentation for IDoc Types
F110	Parameters for Automatic Payment (AP Payment Program)
F111	Parameters for Payment of PRequest (Treasury Payment Program)

Table 10.6: Miscellaneous transaction codes

ESPRESSO TUTORIALS

You have finished the book.

A The Authors

Mary Loughran has been specializing in the SAP Financials area since 1997 and has worked with numerous clients throughout North America and Europe in the areas of Finance and Treasury. She was employed as a consultant with SAP America and was a designated expert within SAP America for Treasury before she left SAP in 2004. From 2004 to 2017, Mary was an independent consultant. In 2017, Mary re-turned to SAP America. Mary's expertise is in the areas of Treasury and Risk Management, In-House Cash, Liquidity Planner, Accounts Payable, payments from SAP in general, Cash Management, and Electronic Banking.

Lennart B. Ullmann has been working in the Cash & Payment management area since 2003. During this time, he has worked as a consultant and project manager on many international SAP Financials projects. He is a specialist in the treasury areas of Payment Management and Bank Communication. Lennart has lived and worked in Germany and in the United States. In his current position, he is the Head of IT Finance for a German DAX company.

B Index

C   Disclaimer

This publication contains references to the products of SAP SE.

SAP, R/3, SAP NetWeaver, Duet, PartnerEdge, ByDesign, SAP Busi-nessObjects Explorer, StreamWork, and other SAP products and ser-vices mentioned herein as well as their respective logos are trademarks or registered trademarks of SAP SE in Germany and other countries.

Business Objects and the Business Objects logo, BusinessObjects, Crystal Reports, Crystal Decisions, Web Intelligence, Xcelsius, and other Business Objects products and services mentioned herein as well as their respective logos are trademarks or registered trademarks of Busi-ness Objects Software Ltd. Business Objects is an SAP company.

Sybase and Adaptive Server, iAnywhere, Sybase 365, SQL Anywhere, and other Sybase products and services mentioned herein as well as their respective logos are trademarks or registered trademarks of Sybase, Inc. Sybase is an SAP company.

SAP SE is neither the author nor the publisher of this publication and is not responsible for its content. SAP Group shall not be liable for errors or omissions with respect to the materials. The only warranties for SAP Group products and services are those that are set forth in the express warranty statements accompanying such products and services, if any. Nothing herein should be construed as constituting an additional warr-anty.

More Espresso Tutorials Books

Lennart B. Ullmann & Claus Wild:

Electronic Bank Statement and Lockbox in SAP® ERP

▶ Processing the Electronic Bank Statement in SAP

▶ Integrating Payment Advices as of SAP EhP 5

▶ New Functionality for Post-Processing as of SAP EhP 6

▶ Detailed Message Monitoring and Reprocessing Examples

http://5056.espresso-tutorials.com

Ann Cacciottolli:

First Steps in SAP® Financial Accounting (FI)

▶ Overview of key SAP Financials functionality and SAP ERP integration

▶ Step-by-step guide to entering transactions

▶ SAP Financials reporting capabilities

▶ Hands-on instruction based on examples and screenshots

http://5095.espresso-tutorials.com

Ann Cacciottolli:

First Steps in SAP® FI Configuration

▶ Get an overview of SAP Financials configuration

▶ Explore fundamental aspects of FI-GL, FI-AR, and FI-AP configuration

▶ Learn how to create, define, and assign company codes and chart of accounts

▶ Obtain hands-on instruction based on examples and screenshots

http://5137.espresso-tutorials.com

Janet Salmon & Claus Wild:

First Steps in SAP® S/4HANA Finance

▶ Understand the basics of SAP S/4HANA Finance

▶ Explore the new architecture, configuration options, and SAP Fiori

▶ Examine SAP S/4HANA Finance migration steps

▶ Assess the impact on business processes

http://5149.espresso-tutorials.com

Reinhard Müller, Frank Rothhaas:

Practical Guide to SAP® FI-RA—Revenue Accounting and Reporting

▶ ASC 606 statutory requirements

▶ Integration between SAP SD, PS, FI-RA, and FI-GL

▶ Troubleshooting data migration challenges

▶ BRFplus in revenue accounting

http://5174.espresso-tutorials.com

Made in the USA
Lexington, KY
23 March 2018